DAEMONS
AND
THE LAW OF ATTRACTION

Daemons
and
The Law of Attraction
Modern Methods of Manifestation

David Thompson

Copyright © 2022 David Thompson

All rights reserved.

TransMudaine Publishing

ISBN: 9780578376752

No part of this book may be reproduced, or stored in a retrieval system, or transmitted in any form or by any means, electronic, mechanical, photocopying, recording, or otherwise, without express written permission of the publisher.

Cover design by: David Thompson

Disclaimer:

None of the material in this book is intended to act as medical, financial, emotional, or lifestyle advice. No material, rituals or suggestions in this book replaces the advice of real medical professionals. The techniques and methods in this book can be used for the treatment of any medical conditions, whether physical, psychological, or emotional, direct or indirect or through implication. The material in this book is not intended to replace the advice of professionals. It is only intended to share spiritual information that is speculative in nature. If you choose to use this material, the author cannot accept any responsibility for the misuse of this information. This material can effect powerful change, use it responsibly.

All images and sigils in this book are original and copyrighted by David Thompson.

To the Goddess Astaroth

Chapter 1 13
   Introduction: The Law of Attraction 13
Chapter 2 18
   Law of Attraction 18
   Real World Results 21
   Defining Your Desire 21
   The Daemons 22
   Daemons are not evil. Period. Full stop. 23
   Common Myths 25
   Real Evil 28
Chapter 3 30
   How Daemons can help with the Law of Attraction. 30
   Pronouncing the Names 31
   Law of Attraction Tools 32
   Vision Boards 32
   Visualizations 34
   Affirmations 35
   Proper Affirmations 37
   Law of Attraction Tools to Discard: 38
   The Rituals 41
   The Paths 42
   Practice Pathworking 44
Chapter 4 47
   Satan 47
   My Experiences with Satan 49
   Working Satan with the Law of Attraction 51
   Standard Invocation 52
   Pathworking 55
Chapter 5 57
   Clauneck 57
   Standard Ritual 58
   Clauneck and the Law of Attraction 59
   Pathworking Clauneck 59
Chapter 6 61
   Astaroth 61
   Astaroth Ritual 62

Astaroth and the Law of Attraction 64
Pathworking Astaroth 64
Chapter 7 66
Seer 66
Standard Ritual 67
Seer and the Law of Attraction 68
Pathworking Seer 69
Chapter 8 71
Flereous 71
Standard Ritual 72
Flereous and the Law of Attraction 73
Pathworking Flereous 74
Chapter 9 76
Verrine 76
Standard Verrine Ritual 77
The Law of Attraction and Verrine 80
Pathworking Verrine 80
Chapter 10 82
Mammon 82
Standard Ritual to Mammon 83
Mammon and the Law of Attraction 84
Pathworking Mammon 84
Chapter 11 86
Lucifuge 86
Standard Ritual 87
Lucifuge and the Law of Attraction 87
Pathworking Lucifuge 88
Chapter 12 90
Marbas 90
Standard Ritual 91
Marbas and the Law of Attraction 92
Pathworking Marbas 92
Chapter 13 94
Volac (also Valac, Ualac, Valax) 94
Standard Ritual 95
Volac and the Law of Attraction 96
Pathworking Volac 96

- Chapter 14 98
  - Law of Attraction Specific Rituals 98
  - Opening Up to Receive 99
- Law of Attraction Rituals for Wealth 101
  - Working the Affirmation 102
  - Making a Vision Board 102
  - Custom Sigil 104
  - Standard Wealth Ritual 105
- Law of Attraction Ritual for Health 109
  - Affirmations 109
  - Vision Board 110
- Law of Attraction Ritual for Love/Relationships 112
  - Sigils and Rituals 114
  - Affirmations 115
  - Vision Board Ideas 115
- Chapter 15 117
  - The New Daemonic Sigils 117
  - Activation 117
  - Satan Sigil 119
  - Clauneck Sigil 121
  - Astaroth Sigil 123
  - Seer Sigil 125
  - Flereous Sigil 127
  - Verrine Sigil 129
  - Mammon 131
  - Lucifuge 133
  - Marbas 135
  - Volac 137
- Appendix 139
  - Hacking the Law of Attraction class 139
  - The ENNS 140
  - Circle Casting 141
  - Color Correspondences 145
  - Days of the week 147
  - Moon Phases 147
  - Helpful Links: 148
  - The Pendulum 149

Activating and Charging your Pendulum 149
Yes/No Chart 150
Complex Sigils Creation 151
About the Author 162

Chapter 1

Introduction: The Law of Attraction

Another book on the Law of Attraction? Seriously? Dude, come on man, another book?

Ooooooooooooooo, man. Okay.

I have been doing what main-stream new Age Folks call "Manifestation" for ages. But it's actually a form of magick. Yes, magick. Speaking weird words and asking for help in drawing to you a desire.

Magick is called a lot of things: "Witchcraft", "Occult", "Chaos magick", "Crack-pot Bovine Excrement", among other terms, some a lot less flattering than that last one.

Well…. the truth is, magick actually works.

What's that? Is there a question in the back? Yes? Go on, speak up!

"Daemons and the Law of Attraction? Mix the two?

Man, I don't know. They have warned me against working with Daemons."

Okay, good question. Here's the answer those who tell you scary stories don't want to hear: Daemons are actually gods that were worshiped in the ancient world,

Therefore, books like this one exist.

When using beings like those in this book, just know your desire will arrive and no one gets harmed. (*Unless that event was already in the works, such as a favorite Great Aunt passing who has you in her will.) The reason for this is that the beings we'll be using in this book are very intelligent, loving celestial beings, who have been labeled "Demons" by various religious orders to frighten people away from working true magick to make their lives better. By doing magick, they no longer needed the priests and churches. If you no longer needed the church, they lose money and power.

Know this: dark beings, beings who cause pain and suffering, DO exist. But those things differ from the beings used in this mode of magick.

What? Okay, another question… Go ahead.

"But, isn't the Law of Attraction" just a bunch of 'Love 'n Light' silliness?"

There are a lot of vocal critics of the Law of Attraction. And many of them are correct.

And the Law of Attraction isn't so much as "watered down" as just incomplete. To market this for the masses, many of whom are phobic of the term "magick", no matter how it's spelled, the Law of Attraction motivational authors and speakers have rebranded magick as "Manifestation".

Go grab any motivational book, such as "Think and Grow Rich", and yeah, there it is. The basic steps to manifest using the oddities of our universal reality, which is considered to be an illusion by many physicists. Go check that out. Here, the internet IS your friend. I'll wait.

So, supposing our reality IS an illusion, then it makes sense that our consciousness can control what happens to us in our life. Manifestation, using the Law of Attraction, says this is the case. Then the books and lectures go off into left field when those authors present methods of tricking your subconscious to altar our reality to manifest a desire.

The key is to fully understand what the Law of Attraction actually is.

The first thing this book will do is redefine the Law of Attraction. Then I'll go over the various methods of altering the Law of Attraction so that it actually works and can be relied upon to actually do all that stuff others say it'll do. For this, you'll be adding an element from traditional magick, summoning a cosmic being to assist you in manifesting your desires.

This book is based upon, but contains different material, than my popular online class I gave in the spring of 2021.

Daemons can be a frightening term for a lot of people. It's confused with "demon" so much, the two are synonymous. But they are very different.

Daemon comes to us from the Greeks, who defined them as Daimon or Daemon (δαίμων: "god", "godlike", "power", "fate"), a term that originally referred to a lesser deity or guiding spirit such as the daimons of ancient Greek religion and mythology and of later Hellenistic religion and philosophy. The word "Daemon" is derived from Proto-Indo-European *daimon which means "provider, divider (of fortunes or destinies)," from the root *da- "to divide".

From this - I often use the term "Daemon" versus the more common spelling of "Demon".

We'll look at the usual daemons I use, plus I'll go into detail on some celestial beings I haven't written about: Satan, Clauneck, Ashtaroth, Seer, Flereous, and several more. Plus, custom sigils for using these Daemons in your magickal work, and how to create a custom sigil to leverage the power of your own higher self with the power of a Daemon.

I'll also give new pathworking summoning methods for each of these beings, which will bring them to you with no need for elaborate rituals or ceremonial workings.

So, need to worry about working this and someone finding your stash of incense, candles, and magick supplies, as this form of magick can be worked in secret if needed.

Chapter 2

Law of Attraction

You have probably read, or at least heard of the book "Ask and It Is Given." I even have that one in my library. It's a good starting spot, but as I've said before, it's incomplete. Decent advice for matching your emotions to your desire, but it never covers how your desires actually manifest. It's pretty skimpy in that category.

I know, because I worked that process for a while, before going back to what worked: Asking particular beings for help in manifesting desires.

The Law of Attraction says that similar thoughts attract similar thoughts. After a while of thinking about your desire, the desire is supposed to manifest. There is a method that uses this to create a fantasy where your dreams are coming true, and as you focus on one thought, soon another thought will arrive, etc.

Possibly the best way of describing how the Law of Attraction actually works is this:

You've just purchased a new car. For the next few days or weeks, it seems you now start seeing cars like yours everywhere. Because your energy and attention are on the car you just purchased, this signaled the energies of our reality and those energies responded by making you notice all similar cars. It's not that there are a lot of cars like yours, it's just that you got "re-tuned" and you just notice all those other cars.

Possibly the BEST description of how it works is while watching TV. Supposed a really, really stupid commercial is shown. It attracts your attention the same way a really nasty person in line at a box store can attract attention. I mean, this commercial uses the most irritating actors possible, if those *ARE* actors, and after the thing ends, you're left wondering what in hell did you just watch. Ugh! After your reaction, the universe will gleefully present that stupid commercial again, and again, and again. Until you turn off the TV and go online. But guess what? It appears in your social media newsfeed. You can't hide from it!

This is the Law of Attraction. To whatever you give your attention, you will attract. Whatever you *EXPECT* to occur **will occur.** (Read that again, it's important to you.)

People who expect to lose their jobs will certainly

lose their job. People who expect to have no money will hardly ever have enough money.

The trick to making the Law of Attraction work FOR you is by shifting what you give attention to, to generate the energy and force necessary to literally alter your reality so that your desire manifests.

And this is where Daemons come in. Most Daemons listed in the Ars Goetia (and other sources) will list an ability is to teach and assist the person calling on them. Your typical Daemon LOVES to help us poor humans in correcting our thought patterns, which have the effect of altering our potential future selves.

I'll cover ten Daemons and how they can help you in manifesting just about anything you really want. These Daemons can also help you figure out what you really need to have manifest, versus a "want". You might want a new sports car, but you NEED a reliable car that can start in winter and doesn't drink too much gasoline.

I'll present pathworking methods for each Daemon, I'll also explain how to work a full ritual so that you can experience the fun involved in having all those candles, incense, sigils, and circles used, and perhaps even spotting the Daemon playing with the incense smoke or manifesting in the circle. (It happens, I get faces in the incense smoke most every time I go into ritual.) Unlike my previous books, which listed detailed rituals, I just give a brief overview of their rituals and then move on to pathworking.

Real World Results

I've been tracking my own results, and the results of my students who have taken the class that this book is based upon. The whole design of this particular book is to get you actual results.

This material was first written several years ago for a class I gave. I did four versions of this class, and after all that, I had even *more* confidence this technique can work, and work easily for anyone.

One student of mine reported back after using these methods, telling me of a tremendous increase in clients and income only a week after starting finishing the class.

One friend of mine had figured the methods didn't work, but then realized her vision board, which incorporated a daemonic sigil and sigil for her wish, had manifested in a way she'd not expected. It was very subtle, the way it appeared.

Defining Your Desire

All of my books have this section.

Most humans struggle to define a desire. So, let's

look at animals. They know what they want. A raccoon, for example, knows what it wants and they tend to be pretty single-minded when it comes to raiding someone's household trash or outdoor cat bowls. The same with a squirrel going after a bird feeder, and even bears have figured out ways to break into houses to raid the pantry. Animals will simply know what they want and they will work to get it. Ask anyone who had to refill a bird feeder about trying to keep a determined squirrel away. I've been dealing with squirrels for a while. Even using special spicy hot bird seed, there was one squirrel who actually loved the stuff, and he emptied the feeder in a matter of hours. I finally gave in and set out special food for the squirrels.

But us humans, even though we can be quite single-minded, still have a hard time actually defining our genuine desires.

Therefore, magick and the Law of Attraction often appear to fail.

One will ask for "XYZ" and your subconscious knows you actually mean you want "ABC", and then when ABC shows up, but you don't immediately recognize that the magick worked.

The Daemons

You might be hesitant to work with this type of being.

Go to most any online community, and you will find horror stories about working with Daemons, dire warnings to avoid them, vague threats of some type of afterlife punishment for just thinking about Daemons.

That is all nonsense.

Mostly, any being you will call upon is actually a piece of a much greater, and higher consciousness energy which created us all, and they behave in a manner that illustrates the Law of Attraction: If you are expecting a trickster being, you will get a trickster being!

Because, remember, the Law of Attraction will bring you what you *expect!*

So, let's try to dispel those expectations right now.

Daemons are not evil. Period. Full stop.

In the past, beings such as nature gods, fertility goddesses, animal gods were used to explain nature. Ancient societies used these gods to insure successful hunts, bountiful crops, victory over enemies, protection of the household, success in business, and a lot more.

These beings also possessed the duality of all nature, both positive/love/good AND negative/fear/evil. Many so-called "devils" were just made-up as a method to frighten people into behaving the way the rulers *wanted* them to behave. Education was actively discouraged, and the religious leaders spread stories to force people into going to the predominant religion in that area. The Kings, dukes, princes, and the churches made sure everyone behaved. They discouraged free thought through various methods, such as torture and executions.

History teaches us it wasn't a good thing to be a freethinker.

The reality is most daemons are out-of-favor gods and goddesses.

Some are personalities of the same being, one part became a saint, the other part a daemon.

Some gods were actual spirits incarnating into human form, who eventually broke out of the restrictions of our reality, and became what many call "Ascended Masters". (More about that in my Grecian Magick books.)

When monotheism swept across the land, all the elder gods and out of fashion angels were re-imagined into being "demons" or - with one religion - saints. They discouraged people from working with the "demons".

If you spend any time at all looking up Daemons, you'll run across several books that date from the middle ages. In these texts, you will find many daemons, with some outlandish descriptions, and drawings of the sigils and instructions on how to protect yourself from the Daemons, etc. The hierarchy of Daemons is pulled directly from Feudal

Europe, with Kings, Dukes, princes, and the occasional President. Looking at any of the drawings, I have to ponder what they were doing when the being appeared to them, and if, perhaps, the Daemon was having a bit of a joke on the magician.

"Hey, watch this! I'm going to appear to this guy like a three-headed dragon!"

"Oooo. Make one head look like old King Oglaf. He was a right smarmy bastard!"

"Perfect! Then I'll speak in a high, squeaky voice!"

And then they all laughed.

I just know this is what happened. It became a contest among the Daemons to see who could come up with the most bizarre image to manifest. That's the only explanation I can come up with to explain why Bune would appear as a three-headed dragon, or Bael an enormous spider with the heads of a man, cat, and frog. They awarded extra points to Bael for the pointed ears on the man's head.

The only other plausible is that the magicians were getting into the good drugs and were experiencing acid-like hallucinations.

Common Myths

Myths and misinformation surround Daemons. If you look at current events, you can see the mechanizations of "demonizing" at work:

They'll steal your soul.

First off, a soul is an integral part of the human system, a merging of spirit and physical in a material vessel. Yes, you can get cut-off from your own spirit, however it can't be separated from you. By "cut-off" I mean your spirit is still there. It's just that your physical brain and consciousness have lost touch with it. You can no longer hear your inner soul communicating with you.

Since there is, in reality, NO HELL, no place of sulfur and fire, and even if it existed, a soul cannot feel physical pain, your soul cannot "go to hell" because of committing some sin in the eyes of some deity. Lakes of burning brimstone would not harm or hurt your soul. Religious leaders who were trying to scare you into following their narrative created sin and hell.

Selling your soul.

No. See my answer to stealing a soul. It's silly.

It's a popular myth. I hear about these fears all the time. I have wondered what exactly a good used soul goes for these days, and is there a dealer mark-up book for a soul, like a car? Seriously, what's the going rate for a gently used soul, only driven on weekends to and from the bingo hall? Low mileage, lots of extras, power windows and door locks.

Yes, selling your soul is silly.

Backfiring or Rebounding magick.

This one is a real possibility. It usually only occurs when one is working magick to control another person. This is where we get into that sticky "free-will" stuff, and it needs a good, long looking into before working this type of magick.

Curses fall into this category. I have seen people who've been attacked by magick and when they fight back, the other practitioner will complain about their magick backfiring. Well, you're just the target of someone fighting back. This is like a bully crying to the teacher because Timmy had fought back and delivered a hard punch to his jaw after being bullied for days or weeks.

Sometimes magick will rebound because the desire is simply not going to happen, no matter how badly you want it. As in, that guy will not leave his wife and kids for you, no matter how much magick you aim at him. I have literally had a daemon tell me, straight up, the magick would not work, nope, not at all. When I was working a ritual for a friend who was in love with a guy who was married. In the ritual, the daemon made it clear this was a waste of magick energy. In these cases, the magick simply will make you feel worse, as your desire will not be showing up as requested. It leads to further heartbreak and is not recommended.

Possession.

Another popular myth.

In horror movies and books, a demon is often to blame for the events around someone who is supposed to be possessed. Rarely, these stories use an actual Daemon, and it's often an ancient god or demon, such as Pazuzu. Pazuzu certainly looks scary, but he's just another disrespected god.

Simply working with a specific Daemon will not subject you to the risks of possession. The entities who WILL possess humans are those I have spoken about before: True dark entities.

Real Evil

Real evil can be easily found in humans. Throughout history, humans have unleashed real horrors and evil against their fellow humans.

In my previous book on Daemons, I went over some examples of real demons I have encountered, and what I think they may be, so this section will be kept short.

Simply put: Yes, real evil things exist. Yes, many call them "demons", which is why I use "daemon". These things are dark, lower vibrational energy, and will often poke into our reality via portals or wormholes. Once here, they will feed upon our energy, preferring the energy of fear and anger. These things are energy vampires, and they can cause pain, fear, and fighting. Once they latch onto a human, they will keep feeding on that fear and the energy of fear and anger all the people around the victim.

I have seen these. I have banished them.

But these things are NOT Daemons.

Please do not confuse the two or allow anyone to tell you differently.

Chapter 3

How Daemons can help with the Law of Attraction.

Unlike other books on LOA and on Daemons, this book will merge the two into a complete process. You will use "Vision Boards" and specific pathworkings to tie your LOA desire to the magick of a specific daemon.

These spirits have all agreed to be part of this book.

We will be using Daemons to *assist* us in working the Law of Attraction. We will ask them to adjust our vibrational patterns to match that of our desire. We will surround ourselves with the images of our desire and the sigil of the Daemon. These images will be "hidden in plain sight" so as to avoid the inevitable discovery by "muggles", people who will scoff and try to tell you that magick doesn't work, people who will literally cause your magick to fail with their own pessimistic reactions to your symbols of magick.

There will be no pentagrams or pentacles, no easily

recognizable icons of any of the Daemons.

The new Daemon sigils I've designed for this book will appear only as interesting lines and shapes to others. These are abstract images tied to each being. This means that you can openly display these sigils and no one around you will recognize them, unless you call attention to them!

Pronouncing the Names

Want to witness a complete meltdown and some real flaming replies? Go onto any online group or forum, and ask about pronouncing the names of various Daemons. Everyone has their own way of pronouncing the names, and no two are alike.

I tend to just say the same as close to how it's spelled as possible, and the *Daemon* always arrives. What does this tell you? The beings really don't care how you say their names, as long as you summon them with sincere effort, and with good intentions.

Again: **They Do Not Care** how the name is pronounced. Many of these beings come from a time before written or spoken language, and they were summoned by many different names across the eons of history, both written and unwritten history.

The last thing you need to worry over is how to say their names or ENNs. If a daemon has a particular way they'd prefer you to day their name, they'll let you know.

Law of Attraction Tools

Years ago, I had a model over for a shoot, mostly for a stock agency. It was a typical casual shoot, and afterwards, the model sat with me by my computer as we reviewed the images. She looked up and saw a bulletin board over my workspace. I usually put up photo ideas, cartoons, etc. In one corner was a small piece of poster board with the things I wanted to manifest.

She goes, "Oh, you have a vision board!"

I nodded and asked if she was into manifesting. I didn't know her well enough to talk about my more advanced practices of magick. "How's it working for you?" I asked.

"Ugh! I'm still working on it!"

This should tell you that many people will work the Law of Attraction, but with very limited success. It's almost as if the desired manifestations only appear by accident. And it's not because there is a lack of effort!

This is why I wrote this book.

Vision Boards

I use vision boards as a tool in many areas. As a photographer, I keep a spot with photo ideas. As a writer, I use a vision board to sketch out plots, characters, scene ideas.

For magick, I use a vision board to assist me in defining what it is that I want.

Law of Attraction gurus typically teach about vision boards, but they add stuff like "This, or something better!" to the board. I remember doing that.

And that, dear reader, is where it all goes pear-shaped. Nothing appears to work and the vision board is usually shoved to the back of a closet.

In making a vision board, find a drawing or photo of what you want. If you want a car, and feel like adding "This or something better!" then dammit! Cut out a photo of the better car and use it!

Take your time working on this. And note that sometimes, in little devious ways, these vision boards will actually work. I will add sigils I've made for my desire to the vision board, and I will include any other sigils that connect to beings I am using to manifest that desire.

Use any method you wish to attach the images. Make sure it's secure. You don't want photos or sigils dropping to the floor after a few weeks. I use white glue mostly, sometimes a glue stick. With a glue stick, go with a good brand. For money, find a gold glitter glue stick and outline the images of money with it.

And keep each vision board to a single desire. Don't

confuse the energy by asking for a house AND car on the same board.

Like I mentioned above, when I was doing photography, I'd often pull images to use. These are called "mood boards" and give everyone on the photo team the style and general feel of the images we were going to produce.

In 2001, I kept seeing this awesome model, so I pulled a lot of images of her. Holy cow, this model is tall, blonde, a figure guaranteed to cause cardiac arrest in male over the age of 60. The type of blonde to make mere mortal men do stupid shit, like let go of the controls of their life and fly into the side of a mountain.

Fast forward to 2016, and I had a script that needed an east European woman as a vampire. I was just surfing the web, and I spotted that SAME MODEL again. This time I noted she had started acting. I dug around and sent her an email. She responded and read the script and was on board as that vampire after a lunch meeting at Canter's Deli in LA's Fairfax district. Sure, it took a few years, but the desire to meet this very same model actually manifested.

Visualizations

Often listed as a LOA tool, visualizing is very, very important in making magick work. In all my magick books and classes, the key element is always visualizing the results occurring.

In each ritual, I have you stop and visualize. Practicing this is very easy, it's just a daydream where you see what you wish to have happen.

Now, why doesn't every daydream actually happen? Why don't sex-addled boys get their crush? I mean, if a daydream fantasy is a way to manifest, why isn't that boy dating the hot cheerleader?

This is where working magick steps in. During the ritual, you channel energy, energy from you and from the beings you summon, and it is directed towards making your desire manifest.

It is with this push of energy that actually causes that daydream vision to manifest.

Affirmations

Another tool which also seems to work every once in a while, especially when used by itself.

I had this book, which focused only on the affirmation aspect of Law of Attraction. It walked you through each step of how an affirmation should be written. I forget how many of these I wrote and read out loud. Many would be phrased to sound like a pattern rhyming.

The issue was, at each step, they advised you to add certain phrases. Phrases which typically cause real magick to

NOT work.

Time constraints, like "in its own perfect time…". "This or something better" conditional statements. Giving thanks, which is a good practice in all magick, but usually done in magick to thank the Daemon or God who has agreed to help you. I mean, these affirmations eventually got quite lengthy.

More conditions were being added, such as arriving safely and harming none. Which is, in and of itself, a good thing. But my advice is that when working with Daemons, don't do this. They are highly evolved beings and they simply do not work in any manner that will cause harm to anyone, which is why you can't use them for curses.

Then, like in doing novenas to Angels or Saints, you're told to work the affirmations daily for quite a while, often over the course of twenty days.

Phew.

It's almost as if the "Universe" grants you the desire just to shut you up. Like a parent being worn down by a kid asking for a toy. "Here, now shut up!"

The Universe hates nagging people. I know I do!

But there is a way to use affirmations to achieve actual results. Which is why I advise keeping this tool handy.

Except it works differently. Like my Book of Life, this method needs a special book and pen. You simply choose a notebook to be the special book, with a special pen. You write what you wish to manifest in a phrase that is using active verbs. Write as if it's happening NOW, not in the future.

Proper Affirmations

Shhh. This is a secret. But here's a fast set of instructions on making simple affirmations work for you. Ready? Okay, here we go:

1. Ask for something you KNOW you can accomplish. Start small, and work up.
2. Do not add ANY conditions!
3. Write the Affirmation in the book. Imagine that your special pen is a magick wand, and as you write in the book, those desires begin to take shape, forming in space, and then pushing into our world in physical form.
4. Close the book. Then put the book away. Maybe open the book once a day and just gaze at the affirmation, then put it away.
5. Keep the affirmation a SECRET. Don't go blabbing to everyone about how you are manifesting "XYZ."

And that's it. It works.

Easy. I hear you saying, "Yeah, but almost too easy..." And that's one key, it is why it easily works.

When you work with a Daemon and use your Affirmations book, it's even easier. Plus, it is okay to use one Daemon on one page, and a different Daemon on another. Put one affirmation on a page, tied to Clauneck, and on the next page over, you can write an affirmation using Flereous or another Daemon.

By adding the energy of a Daemon, these affirmations become quite strong. After writing out the affirmation, there's no reason to even look back. Close the book, put it away somewhere safe, then go on about your day. Don't even think about it.

Law of Attraction Tools to Discard:

Acting "As If"

Uh huh. Right. Easier said than done. I've been there, under such stress and pressure, it's a wonder ANY of my magick was successful.

Let's say you are living in a horrible environment and desperately need to escape that situation. When you are immersed in negative energy, in a fearful state of mind, it's damned hard to elevate your emotional set-point to that of one who is NOT living in fear and negativity.

I often say that it's very difficult to manifest when you are in a state of panic until I learned some Daemons are very good at helping in these circumstances. Just enough of the magick happened it sent waves of relief through me which triggered the rest of the magick to work.

As you can see, asking Satan for help even while in a state of fear can eventually lead to much better things.

The biggest issue for you might be some elements of fear of working with a being, such as Satan. Unless you grew up in an open-minded household, where stories of "the devil" or of "demons" trying to lure you into hell, then I advise you to consider using another being at first. It's just that Satan has such an evil reputation outside the magick community. It might be better to work with another being initially.

(Oh yes, Satan *isn't* Lucifer. Two different beings. Satan isn't the devil, either. In fact, there is no actual "devil", just certain beings who have been transformed into a "devil".)

My advice is to work with another being, and summon Satan a few times to have him just visit you. That's right, you don't have to summon a Daemon only when you wish to ask for assistance; it's a common practice among many magick practitioners to summon beings just to feel their energy, ask questions, get guidance presenting no requests or petitions.

Ask and It Is Given

Oh, don't even go there. I mean it. Who are you asking? The Universe? Asking a god? At last count, there are over twelve thousand deities scattered around our world, so which one are you asking? Any old god or being who just happens to be passing by?

Imagine if you were on a pleasant walk around a neighborhood, and at each house, the person there stops you to ask for a favor. Maybe at one house, you'll stop and agree to help, but you can't help everyone around the neighborhood.

So, in this method, we pick ONE being to ask.

Emotional Set-points and Vibrational Matching

This is another Law of Attraction coaching issue. I see bunches of people being coaches, helping people with their emotions and proper vibrational matching.

An entire cottage industry revolves around this stuff. Books, DVDs, live workshops. Folks are making tons of money doing this, and from where I stand, it seems to be the major focus of all the coaches.

Nothing wrong with this, but it's the only aspect they work on, and if you can't work it, it's a lack of meditation or you don't want the desire enough. In my teachings, if a student is having trouble, we try to get to the root of the issue. Which is where my ability to hear the spirits and look at the complete picture allows me to assist the student in manifesting their desires.

The Rituals

Each Daemon can be summoned using a basic High Magick ritual, which I will outline in this segment. When working ritual magick, it's more about you and your preferences than what is written in magick books. The beings in this book can differ on what they prefer as an offering, and some daemons might ask for a blood offering, but most won't.

How you work a ritual is all depending on what YOU feel is best.

I set up my altar in my particular way, and you are free to set up YOUR altar in any way that suits you.

The basic ritual is:

Light incense and candles.
Turn out room lights.
Cast your circle (if you use a circle)
Work the ritual.
Close the ritual.
On with room lights.

If using incense on a piece of charcoal, allow it to burn out.

Extinguish candles.

If using a specific candle for the spell, make sure it can burn safely until it goes out.

After a day, dispose of any offerings.

That is really all there is to this. No special phrases to chant, no intricate dances to perform, no skulking around cemeteries in the dead of night, all that is optional. But maybe having an animal familiar around is cool.

The Paths

Ask any practitioner of magick about pathworkings, you will probably get many answers. Some define pathworking far differently than I define it.

For me, it's a series of visualizations to assist you in attuning your energy system to match that of the being you wish to summon. It is those images I will share with you in this book.

How they work? Each image sets up your mind to a specific pattern, which then matches the energy patterns of the being you are summoning. It puts you on an even level with the being.

Don't worry if you don't feel any difference when you work on a series of visualizations. Don't worry that you might not be fully working the visuals, as all you need is a few seconds of the image for it to trigger the energy match.

Once you have visualized each image, the Daemon is with you. It's calling to them using a technique that I have seen to work, and work quite well. I have given several friends this method, and they all report good progress.

If you are having trouble maintaining focus, just go slow. Practice. Practice just sitting, with no thoughts. A quiet, meditative state will work wonders in calming an over-active mind.

And keep practicing. Visualizing is something we all did as children. Playing "make-believe". Daydreaming and tuning out were forced out of us while we grew into adulthood.

It's perfectly okay if you drift off and find yourself asleep while working the practice visualizations. This means your body needed rest, and it took advantage of your quiet mind to drop off. It happens to me as well.

With a little practice, pathworking can be done most anytime, except while doing a task that requires perfect concentration. Don't do this while driving a car, or operating any other large machine. During a family gathering, I have worked pathworking rituals in the living room. I did one while waiting for a flight at the airport. I focused on a free upgrade. Which occurred just minutes after the ritual was worked.

Practice Pathworking

To get the full effect of pathworking, I'll suggest some practice you can work on, daily if possible, that will assist you in tuning your mind to getting the visuals and keeping those visuals until you are finished working with the Daemon.

To begin, sit in a very comfortable chair, lights dimmed, but not off. Make sure all sources of interruption are silenced (Parents, good luck with this one. I suggest while they're at school or down for a nap.)

Once you know you won't be disturbed, settle down and work this relaxation exercise.

- Breathe deeply, in and out, three times
- Close your eyes
- Slow, steady breaths
- Shut out any stray thoughts you might have
- Think of any of the following scenes:
    - A sunny day in a park.
    - Floating on a cloud, seeing the

countryside below you.
- A loved one smiling at you.
  ◦ Try to hold each visual as long as you can. Go INTO the visual. Try to feel the sensations of each scene.
  ◦ Breathe deeply.
  ◦ Then, let it all go.

Try to find time to do this every day, and after about a week, or ten days, the pathworkings will be much easier to work.

Sigils

In this book, we'll make use of sigils created to manifest your desire. My High Magick 101 book covers the creation of a sigil, plus my High Magick workbook contains multiple worksheets to assist you in creating a specific sigil for your desire.

Using a sigil with the Law of Attraction means you will need to condense your affirmation into a shorter phrase, tied to a specific Daemon, in order to create your sigil. It's easier than you think.

Your desire plus asking the Daemon to assist in bring it to you. Put into a phrase such as "I ask that [Daemon's Name] brings to me…. (your desire)." Again, very, very easy. You do not need to spend hours or days in meditation, holding your hands "just so", while trying not to think of anything.

Nah.

More on this later. Let's look at the Daemons we'll be using for this!

Chapter 4

Satan

Ave Satanis!

"Hail Satan!" roughly translated. And there is a lot to give him thanks for in my experience.

I'll skip the debates on whether Satan is a male or female. To me, Satan shows up as male energy. He is routinely summoned when I am doing a full ritual, as it's part of the banishing and circle casting I use.

I initially used the most commonly found sigil for Satan, then I began using a simplified sigil before finally designing the one I present in this book. A simple search will often bring up the image of Baphomet, who most definitely isn't Satan, and the sigil of Lucifer, which appears like some corporate logo.

Satan is often confused for Lucifer by many people, and there is some discussion (*) whether the two are aspects of a single being, or two names for the same being. In my workings, these two are very different. Where I will summon and work with Lucifer on business and wealth matters, I turn to Satan when I need solutions to personal issues and a clear path forward.

Satan is good for general magick, and has provided quick results when I have petitioned him. I'll be going into more detail about Satan and the Law of Attraction than the others listed in this book, and the same concepts can apply to the other Daemons, except for Verrine. We'll burn that bridge when we cross it.

Doing a standard ritual is suggested when first beginning work with the top dog of all daemons. Make sure you have a correct sigil or pentagram if all you have are the Luciferian or Baphomet sigils. He'll STILL respond to those other symbols, but his energy isn't as strong as it would usually be if using the correct symbols.

After the initial ritual, basically a meet-and-greet, talk to him about what you wish to accomplish in the future. He'll gently guide you. After the initial contact, you can then move over to the pathworking method of summoning Satan.

If you have never worked with Satan, or you harbor any fear at all, know that he will never harm you or another person. There is no need for "protection" circles or calling in angelic guardians. Satan as "The Devil" is a recent bastardization of the true Satanic being given to us by mainstream religions and the media.

If Satan was really as dangerous as they let on, then there'd be a lot of independent writings about this, by people who are not followers of any organized religion. Anyone who has an agenda, wanting you to work with their own system, will often "demonize" working with daemons, especially Satan.

I have had several students tell me that another guru had warned them against "mixing their magick" with any other work, or the beings they're using will get angry if you used any other beings. Sounds like they've joined with the deity known as YHWH, Jehovah, who is the god of Abraham in the Old Testament, and is quite a jealous god. Avoid those gurus. If their god is a jealous being, that is no loving god. It's a projection of the jealousies of the guru and not an actual deity. Not one I'd ask around, honestly. Give me Lucifer or Satan. I know what to expect, and it's not fear or jealousy.

My Experiences with Satan

The very first time I ever worked ritual magick, it was a ritual outlined in an old book my mom had brought home from the library. It had a chapter entitled "Love and Sex Magick for Men". Being a horny fifteen-year-old, I went right to that chapter. One ritual involved using Satan. And drawing symbols with your blood, plus the target's name.

It didn't work.

Perhaps I'm lucky it didn't work. I was too young to understand the powers of Satan and how those powers come with responsibility. When you align yourself with his powers, just about anything is possible. Much later, I discovered another similar book on magick and in it were several rituals to Satan. This time, I worked a small ritual to bring a specific person back into my life.

This time, it worked.

This ritual wasn't nearly as involved as the one I worked to Satan when I was a teenager. That is the key to why this one worked: it was simple, straightforward, and easy to work. In less than a week, I was in a club that had just opened up. I was still young, the world not nearly as screwed up as it is now, and I was going out a lot. This was also when every time you moved, you had a new phone number. I'd lost contact with this woman and wanted to see her again.

I spotted the woman who I had wanted to meet with again. She was working as a waitress in this club, and she spotted me and walked right towards me. I got her new number, and she was over at my place in just a few days later.

I worked this one again when I'd moved back to Austin, newly divorced and wanted to meet up with a model

I'd lost contact with. Again, it worked.

Every time I have worked a simple ritual to Satan, it's worked. A more elaborate ritual also brings results. Of all the beings I've ever worked with, Satan is 99% effective.

Working Satan with the Law of Attraction
One could wonder how Satan (as well as the others) can assist with manifesting using the Law of Attraction. Does this take a ritual to Satan, with blood offerings? Do you have to wear a black robe and perform the ritual under a full moon in a graveyard at midnight?

As much fun as that last scene appears, using Satan to supercharge your Law of Attraction manifestations is quite easy, and can hide in the open. (My favorite magick technique, BTW)

Hiding your magick in plain sight takes very little effort. Satan's sigil can be incorporated into a vision board as a piece of artwork. I have designed Satan's new sigil to be easily worked into images that reflect what you wish to manifest.

After working the exercises for pathworking, you work the Law of Attraction visualizing, visualize the images needed to summon Satan, then show him the visuals, and ask for help in manifesting that desire.

Add Satan to the Affirmations in your special book. It

can be phrased as simply, "Satan now brings to me (your desire). And for this, I thank him!" Then add Satan's sigil to the affirmation.

If you are stuck on defining your desire, then you can summon Satan to join with you and ask him how best to define your desire. I have had instances where I was manifesting a specific goal, and during a standard ritual to Satan, he said I'd be better off by asking for X, as it'll easily lead to the desired result. I shifted my desire, and the manifestation occurred in a matter of days.

Standard Invocation

As written in my other books, there is a traditional method of Daemonic invocation, which is a gentler method of summoning Satan than the usual Goetia-based rituals. You won't be "binding" the spirit, and you won't be ordering the spirit around.

I include this ritual only to outline what a typical ritual to a Daemon might comprise, prior to working the Law of Attraction using daemons.

Organize your altar as you see fit.

I use white and black candles as my altar candles. Both to "set the mood" and provide light during the ritual.

I will then use a silver candle as a dedicated candle to Satan.

I use an incense burner with frankincense, but you

can use what you have on hand. Satan isn't picky about incense.

I have his sigil (the one I designed) in the center of the altar, and I have the offering bowl to one side, and a fireproof bowl on the other side, because I will burn the petition and sigil for my desire during the ritual. If this is involving a blood offering, I have a diabetic lancet handy, and a small printed sigil for the blood offering.

I light the altar candles, and the incense. Room lights go out and the ritual starts.

Once all the invocations are out of the way, and I feel the other beings have arrived, I now summon Satan. When working this ritual, I omit the last invocation in the basic ritual, since I am already summoning Satan. No need to work his summoning several times.

I say his ENN, "Tasa reme laris Satan – Ave Satanis" three times, because there is something about saying it three times that seems to work. I have run rituals where I just said the ENN once, and that works, but three is the number that always works. (Maybe they take a bit to respond, as if I'd caught them in the daemonic restroom and they needed to finish.)

Pause a few moments, then see if you can detect his energy anywhere near you. It's okay if you can't, just know he's hovering nearby. Use a pendulum if you want to have easy-to-understand answers to simple questions. (Full directions in the Appendix)

Satan always arrives with no elaborate manifestations. I just feel his energy enter my circle to the right, and it drifts around to my left. There he stays until I address him. I hear him in my mind, and I don't need to use a pendulum to communicate with him.

He'll be frank with me about the desired outcome of any ritual. He's told me on three occasions what I was asking for couldn't be delivered as requested. Especially if the ritual is for a client, and the energy just isn't right.

Satan will also tell me when his energy isn't the right energy for a specific desire. He'll tell me I'd be better off asking another being to assist in the manifestation of a desire. He is the ONLY being who has ever advised me in this fashion.

"You want Lucifuge to help with this one, he'll get you faster results," was an answer I'd gotten several months ago when I was working a ritual to ensure the success of a class I wanted to write. I nodded and took a break and found the other sigil and the resulting class eventually became the basis for this book!

Why does Satan do this? He's a spirit of great strength, but sometime your inner energy will resonate better with another spirit, thus bringing better results.

Other Daemons will either agree to the petition, or they'll not agree, but they rarely suggest alternatives to the ritual. The worse that has happened is that the Daemon simply did not help to manifest the desire. Nothing happened.

When things go wrong in magick, this is the outcome 99% of the time.

So you should seek a psychic reading for why magick fails. The answer could be anything, but the only way to know is by *ASKING*. Divination using a psychic, a tarot deck, or even a pendulum to help you figure out what went wrong.

Pathworking

Contacting Satan via pathworking is a very simple. Don't be fooled how simple this is.

Initially, work a regular ritual to make first contact, then let him know you intend to use this pathworking method for future rituals. This way, you'll already be familiar with his energy and can detect him when he arrives for future work.

Chose a place and time where you will not be disturbed.

Quiet your mind. Shut out any distracting thoughts. You may wish to turn off the room lights and work in darkness. Or you can simply shut your eyes.

Two deep breaths.

Now visualize the following scenes in your mind. Make them as real as possible.

- A warm gust of air on your face.
- Soft sand under your feet. The sand stretches to the horizon. The sand is bright white.
- The sky is a deep blue.
- A shimmering in the air in front of you.

At this point, Satan has arrived. Communicate to him what you wish to have occur, or simple communicate with him, getting answers and guidance in your affairs.

Do Daemons need offerings or sacrifices when doing pathwork? "Sometimes" is the best answer I have. I often will give an offering once results manifest. I will pour a small shot-glass of whiskey and sit it on Satan's sigil. Allow at least 24 hours before pouring out the whiskey. It's best to pour it on the ground outside. With all distilled spirits, don't pour this into a potted plant.

Chapter 5

Clauneck

Clauneck is not a traditional daemon in The Lesser Key of Solomon, but he appears in multiple magick texts, and is spoken often in texts such as Dictionnaire Infernal. He is described as a Turkish spirit who has power over goods, wealth, gold and was often used in pacts. According to many sources, he is "best loved" by Lucifer.

Some sources have Clauneck being a good daemon to call upon to get honest feedback on which of your dreams to focus upon, and which to discard. He'll straight up tell you if you're wasting your time. He'll also let you know about your shortcomings, so be prepared.

A few years ago, I summoned Clauneck and asked about a film I was developing. He flat-up told me to ditch the person who wanted to produce the project. I hesitated and in a few months; it was apparent that this person really wasn't up to producing a movie.

To many, Clauneck is associated with commerce and building of businesses. Thus, he's a wonderful spirit to call upon when working for yourself. I have not compared Clauneck's working with those of Bune, as I have used him mostly to assist me in matters regarding feedback on projects, such as this book series.

Standard Ritual

Clauneck responds quickly to a traditional ritual, and even a simplified ritual.

His ENN is "Ahvalen Esen Clauneck Kiar" which is repeated three times (as always).

I use frankincense resin, nothing else added.

His planet is Mercury, and I simply go with my basic altar candles, white and black, and a candle for my request.

There are no specific days or times to call on Clauneck, but if you wish, you can call on him on a Wednesday and during the hour of Mercury. Colors to use are a basic black scheme, or shades of oranges. If working with him to remove blocks, use an orange candle.

The offerings I have given him are a small glass of red wine, and on one occasion, I put a drop of blood on his sigil and burned it as offering/sacrifice.

Clauneck and the Law of Attraction

Using affirmations, simply write it such that you are asking Clauneck to help you with obtaining the desire or answer. Write this in your affirmation book, plus his sigil.

Work your affirmation into a sigil, using any method you prefer, and build a vision board around that sigil. If you make a sigil using the letters, perhaps cut those letters out of magazines or newspaper, and create a sigil like you would a collage. Just don't paste the letters like it's a ransom note from an old TV movie.

On a vision board, incorporate Clauneck by including his sigil or one of the many illustrations that show Clauneck as a man carrying valuables and a gold candlestick.

Pathworking Clauneck

Relax and center yourself.

Once relaxed, visualize the following:

- White sandy beach
- White birds fly overhead
- A pale pink flower in your hand.
- Look up and see a pale mist

At this point, expect Clauneck is near you.

Address him and ask him to assist you. Visualize

what you wish to have happen, and this vision will also be seen by Clauneck. Once you have finished visualizing, ask Clauneck what he might wish. Make a note if he communicates the request for an offering.

Now, you are done, and you can open your eyes.

Chapter 6

Astaroth

Listed (incorrectly) as a Great Duke of Hell, Astaroth is written about in many, many old texts on Daemonology. *Pseudomonarchia Daemonum* places Astaroth next to Beelzebub and Lucifer, creating a "Unholy Trinity". These older texts also switch back and forth between this gentle spirit being a female and a male. Digging deeper, I saw how she came to us from the Phoenicians, the goddess Astarte.

Astaroth is a fascinating goddess, and worth more research at a later date.

Given she is an elder goddess, she contains the same powers as a goddess, such as Aphrodite and Hecate.

Her ENN is "Tasa Alora Foren Astaroth", but I prefer to summon her using phrases to attune her energy to that of Astarte or Inanna, the Mesopotamian goddess of love, beauty, sex, war, justice, and political power.

Being an elder goddess, she is very powerful. Having

her on your side in most any situation almost ensures success, so it's no wonder she was "demonized" by western religions. To be honest, most western religions have issues with the whole sacred feminine goddess concept, and Astaroth is no exception.

Astaroth Ritual

Knowing Astaroth is more of a goddess, and not a daemon, one should take a slightly different approach to summoning her.

Her energy is tied somewhat with Saturn, so I will use a gold candle when summoning her, along with the fragrance of Honeysuckle (if available) or a light, floral scent.

The incense should be frankincense resin, with a stick of another incense for the floral notes.

Overall, her preferred colors are a muted orange, with earthy tones.

She prefers an offering of red, heavy wines, which remind her of her days in ancient Sumer.

No specific moon phase, or hour is needed. Just work her ritual when the time is most convenient for you.

After I cast a circle, I will settle myself and gaze at her sigil. I will allow myself to drop into a slight Alpha state and do some deep breathing.

Then, when I'm ready, I'll say:

- Goddess Astaroth! You who shine so brightly, you rival Lucifer the Light Bringer.
- Goddess Astaroth, you who are known by so many names in so many lands,
- Goddess of Love, Goddess of Beauty, Goddess of power
- I ask that you please join with me in my sacred space.
- I have set aside a sacred spot in my circle.
- Join with me! Grace me with your powerful presence.

Keep an eye on the incense. She will often signal her presence by making the smoke drift around, often against any slight draft that may in the room. The candle may also flicker.

At this time, I will read any petition I may have, then I will give over the offering.

Spend some time in meditation, seeing your desire manifesting.

Once you have meditated for at least a minute, the ritual is over.

Ask her to depart as follows:

Goddess Astaroth, I thank you for being here with

me, and I ask that you please depart, as this ritual is at an end. Again, I thank you for coming into my space. Good bye until I next call.

And that's it.

Astaroth and the Law of Attraction

Incorporating Astaroth into the Law of Attraction starts with her new sigil. It's a simple design that you can easily put into a vision board and hang somewhere.

Given her connection to the elder goddesses, she's perfect to manifest a family, safe birth of a child, and to help make a home garden lush and green. She'd be the go-to goddess for casting a veil of glamor over you to attract that new special person into your life, or to spice up an already existing relationship.

Using affirmations, incorporate Astaroth's energy by rewording your petition into an affirmation, then draw her sigil below the affirmation in your book.

On a vision board, use her sigil as a central focus to tie her energy to that of the images on the board.

Pathworking Astaroth

As always, ensure you won't be disturbed and settle in and calm yourself, deep breaths, slow and deep.

When ready, close your eyes and visualize the following:

- An open country garden.
- The smell of fresh flowers. Watch as a Honeysuckle blooms, and opens up.
- Bluebirds land on a branch above you. See its red breast and bright blue back.
- A warm, fresh breeze hits your face.

The goddess Astaroth will appear to you in this garden. Call to her, send a welcoming energy towards her.

Address her and state your request. See if she nods or speaks to you. Make a note of how she appears to you.

Once you're finished, visualize your desire manifesting. Go into detail, taking your time.

After you've fully visualized what you wish to have happen, bid the goddess farewell, and open your eyes.

The ritual is completed.

Chapter 7

Seer

Seer, sometimes spelled "Seere", is a Goetic daemon, listed as a "Prince", with a nice following of demons. He's at number 70.

I first encountered Seer while looking for beings to help me with a very specific problem: I needed someone to see my point of view on a project, and they were very resistant to my efforts to bring them around to my point of view. Seer is good at removing obstacles, and this disagreement was an obstacle.

I worked that ritual, and the person did eventually agree, but that ultimately didn't solve the problem. The problem was solved when this person left the project, because the obstacle went away!

Seer has many abilities, as do all the Daemons, but he excels in making things move forward and clearing the path. He can make you more productive as well, allowing you to work without interruption (which I use when I am finishing a book!)

Use Seer for these purposes, but you can also ask him to work on other issues. Seer is good at leading to you wealth, if asked correctly. He will not bring the wealth to you, but will guide to on the correct path. The rest is up to you.

Standard Ritual

Notice what I wrote earlier about asking Seer correctly. Seer doesn't seem to react very well to demanding petition. Use respect and approach him like he's one of those old-fashioned uncles. Say "please" and "thank you" and use "sir". As in "Lord Seer, please assist me in obtaining great wealth, lead me in your well-known manner, and I am ready to follow. Thank you, Lord Seer!" is a good template to follow.

Seer's ENN is "Jeden et Renich Seer tu tasa" spoken three times. Then you say "Seer please be with me" and he'll arrive.

Seer is happy with any incense you decide to use, and the colors are up to you.

Ritual timing: Anytime. Or you can calculate based upon the goal you wish to manifest, then go with that color. Gold or silver for wealth (see my High Magick 101 book on this), orange for road clearing, green for luck, etc.

Offerings: Alcohol like whiskey or scotch, red wine, raw egg.

Basic ritual stuff now, the circle casting, expelling of negative energies, figuring out which way is north. If you feel the need to do the old calling in the elements and Daemons for each element, then summon Seer.

After summoning Seer, read your desire out loud, in the form of a petition. Stay quiet for a moment or two, and see if you can hear his reply.

After the offering, shut everything down and after 24 hours, place the offering outside. If giving alcohol, pour it onto rocks, and not the plants.

That's it.

Be mindful of any intuitive nudges, sending you in the right direction.

Seer and the Law of Attraction

Pattern all your LOA work using Seer after the one for Satan. Being mindful of how to address him, word any Affirmation using his title or "Lord". He's really a stickler for us using this title, so please do so and then enjoy his effective magick. His most common form when appearing is a man on a winged horse, so you can use those images on a vision board.

Since the image of a Pegasus, which is a winged horse, is associated with fantasy, you can combine the horse with other elements that represent your desire, and tie Seer's energy to the goal of a vision board.

You can craft a sigil using a simplified version of the Affirmation, and place that on a vision board as well.

Pathworking Seer

As always, find a spot where you can relax and visualize without being disturbed.

- Blue sky overhead with puffy white clouds.
- A gust of wind sending leaves circling around you.
- A grassy area with a large boulder in the center
- You are next to the boulder
- You watch a beautiful winged horse graze in the grass.

Keep the image of the boulder in your mind. Seer will now appear. Speak with him, ask him for help, then visualize the outcome of your desire arriving.

Give thanks to Seer for his help.

David Thompson

Let the image of the horse vanish. You're now done.

Chapter 8

Flereous

This Daemon is sometimes known as Fereous or Haures. He's number 64 on the Ars Goetia hit parade, but don't let the idea of him being number 64 fool you. He's quite useful and powerful.

(Also note, some consider Flereous to be a feminine spirit, but I get a neutral energy, so Flereous could be or both.)

He is often summoned while casting a circle using the traditional methods, as he represents the element Fire, and is summoned while facing south.

I will often summon Flereous when I need direction for my business or in life. He'll give you straight answers and doesn't sugarcoat it. I once had him tell me to forget a specific photography endeavor, as it'd not work out. Well, I went ahead anyway. And yeah, I got very little business. So... I summoned him again, and he told me to work on teaching classes and writing these books. Then he gave me assistance in my writing, giving me the inspiration to write, and helped improved my skills at both writing and self-editing.

So, if you are a writer, he's a good Daemon to make a pact with (See my Daemons of High Magick to see how this is done).

A couple of other things Flereous is good at is sabotaging a business rival, cause mishaps to happen to others, so he might come in handy for assisting in any Karmic actions you may need to take. (*1)

Standard Ritual

When crafting a petition to Flereous, be mindful of his abilities and

In any ritual, Flereous loves incense. Especially a mix I did for him.

    1 part each of:

        Frankincense

        Dragon's Blood

        Sandalwood.

That's using resin, of course.

His ENN is "Ganic Tasa Fubin Flereous", which is

---

[1] Be extra careful in working this type of magick, even using the Law of

said three times, followed by asking to join with you.

Use red or gold candles when working a standard ritual to Flereous.

Suggested offerings include raw egg, wine or whiskey, a small bit of fresh beef. He doesn't need a blood offering.

This all works like any other ritual. When casting a circle, if you summon the elements, substitute Samael with his ENN "Sah revenosh ah Samael talau"

Once the space is set, summon Flereous and once you feel he's there, present the petition, and then the offer. It's up to you if you wish to burn the petition.

Once you have completed the ritual, allow the offering to stay on your altar with his sigil for at least overnight. Then dispose of the offering outside. If an egg or piece of meat, some place where wildlife can get to it.

Flereous and the Law of Attraction

Flereous can appear to magicians as a powerful leopard, so I suggest pairing images of leopards with the images of what you wish to manifest, then creating a collage for a vision board.

Use the leopard imagery when crafting an

Attraction. Refer to my warnings about rebound energy in the first chapter.

Affirmation, and in this, ask Flereous's power to be sent into the Affirmations book. Of course, word this affirmation as we've seen in previous Law of Attraction chapters on the other Daemons.

Pathworking Flereous

Set yourself down in a place where you are comfortable, and make sure no one will interrupt you while you work this ritual.

Deep breaths, then close your eyes.
Visualize the following:

- A setting sun, glowing red on the horizon.
- A raven flies overhead, outlined against the red sky.
- A sudden gust of wind at your back.
- A golden orb appears overhead.

Ask Flereous to make himself known to you. Communicate to him what you wish to either ask or speak your request.

He will indicate the answer by either using a pendulum or direct telepathy to guide you as needed. He can literally press against your back to turn you in the right direction.

Once done, give thanks and allow him to depart.

Chapter 9

Verrine

Verrine is a very useful being, and I consider her to be another celestial being who isn't part of the traditional Goetia, but not actually considered a goddess or other being. She is a very helpful being, and very powerful.

I call on her when I need healing. She will help get you (or the person you are seeking to assist) the medical help you seek, often guiding doctors towards an effective treatment. She can also assist you in locating natural treatments for health issues. Some refer to her as preferring holistic approaches to health issues.

In my own experiences, she made it possible for me to get the correct doctors for my ongoing issues, the proper tests, and a treatment plan. I called upon her to aid a friend of a friend with the transition from life to afterlife, assisting the person suffering from end-stages of cancer. This is often the best path forward for someone who is dealing with severe disease. Verrine will visit in astral, and assure the patient that letting go and moving along is in the best interests of their own spirit, and the surrounding people. I have found that people will hang on to this life, usually out of fear of the unknown and out of concern for anyone they might leave behind.

In one instance, Verrine guided the family into finding an end-of-life doula, who assisted everyone in that difficult time.

Standard Verrine Ritual

I'm including this example standard ritual to Verrine since she differs from the other Daemons, being a spirit genius of healing and health.

A normal ritual to Verrine is a lot like any other ritual. For Verrine in specific, you will focus on her element of water, and if using planetary timings, work during the hours of Venus, on the day of Venus (a Friday). See the appendix for a link to a website to quickly calculate this for you)

Her colors are Gold, White, Blue or Green. I have had good luck using mostly blue when working rituals to her. Incense blends can be Lavender, black copal, musk, sandalwood, vetiver, or myrrh.

Offerings for Verrine can be flowers (white or lavender), rosemary, eucalyptus, chamomile, echinacea, or mint, essential oils in a diffuser. Herbs or even clippings from your garden.

If you play music, go with soothing piano pieces. Something usually heard in a calm bookstore will work.

If asking for another person, I'll have their photo and name nearby. Word the petition in any way that is humble, asking for her help. Put a drop or two of a healing oil onto the petition.

Her ENN is "Elan Typan Verrine", spoken three times.

Her name is pronounced to rhyme with "Queen": **Ver-EEN**

The basic ritual is as follows:

Set up your altar in any way that suits you.

Place the altar candles as you see fit. A specific candle to Verrine should be centered, with the incense near or behind the candle. Her sigil is placed in the center of the altar.

Get the main candles going, as well as the incense. Lights off.

Cast a circle. Work any type of banishments you may

feel is necessary.

When that is done, sit and focus on her sigil. Say her ENN three times:

Elan Typan Verrine

Elan Typan Verrine

Elan Typan Verrine

Verrine! Join with me this day. I ask a favor of you!

Read your petition out loud.

At this point in the ritual, light the color candle that is for Verrine. I use a blue chime candle for Verrine, and I have it in a solid glass votive holder, lined with foil.

Verrine! I ask that you charge this candle with your energy! As it burns, your energy is magnified and used to heal (yourself or the target).

Now, time for the offering.

Verrine! In gratitude for listening to my plea, I humble offer you —

Place the offering on the sigil, or if offering a drop of essential oil, drop it on their sigil and allow it to dry.

Take this moment to meditate on the outcome of the ritual. See in your mind how the magick will manifest, yourself or the target of the healing energy becoming well, being restored to full health and able to go about the day without hindrance.

The length of time to meditate isn't fixed. Just take as long as you need to fully visualize. Allow any emotions to arise as well, the joy of feeling healthy or seeing your friend being healed.

The ritual is finished at this point.

Turn the room lights back on and allow the incense to burn out. Make sure the blue candle is in a safe spot and allow it to burn out.

The Law of Attraction and Verrine

Craft a special sigil using your original petition, simplified so that it can make an effective sigil, then use this as a central piece in a vision board.

In your affirmation book, restate the petition as an affirmation, then place her sigil just below the affirmation, visualize the effects of being healed, the proper medical treatment being found, and full health returning.

Pathworking Verrine

Like the previous pathworkings, this one is done when you have a moment for yourself and a clear idea of what you will ask Verrine.

When ready, close your eyes and relax.

- Visualize the following in order:

- A quiet meadow with tall green grass.
- The smell of fresh rain.
- A mist surrounds you.
- Cool and damp on your skin.

Now, Verrine will be near you. Address Verrine and submit your request.

Take a few moments to fully visualize your request manifesting for you. See yourself (or the person you are working this for) feeling better, in full health.

Now, the ritual is done. Ask Verrine to depart, and to please come again when you next call on her.

Chapter 10

Mammon

You might have heard of this one, as he's spoken about in plenty of biblical texts. It appears the word "mammon" was used a great deal in early religious texts and factors in several biblical quotes from Jesus, usually to mean money or wealth.

The being likely started as "μαμμωνᾶ ", which is a Syrian deity, a god of wealth and riches. The word was further personified when Gregory of Nyssa wrote that Mammon was another name for Beelzebub, a Philistine deity associated with Ba'al. In the middle ages, Mammon was further personified as greed and as evil. Thus, again, we have an elder god being turned into something evil.

Mammon resembles the Grecian god, Plutus, who I cover in my Grecian Money Magick book.

I have summoned Mammon as a Daemon multiple times, and in every case, he delivers on my petition. A sudden increase in book sales quickly followed a ritual to him this past summer. Previously, I petitioned him and he delivered a sold-out online class, the class version of this book.

Standard Ritual to Mammon

When working a standard ritual to Mammon, use gold candles, frankincense, and an offering of wine. His ENN is ***Tasa Mammon on ca lirach***, recited three times.

He appears as a wisp of energy, and has rarely taken any recognizable human or animal shape, regardless of the fantastical drawings seen in most texts. He will answer my questions with a definite masculine voice, so I refer to Mammon as "he".

Mammon is also accepting of combine him with either other daemons or even angelic beings, but I have not attempted to combine his energy with that of any god or goddess, although I'd imagine he'd work well with most any Grecian or Roman deity of wealth.

His incense is usually frankincense, which I combine with white opal. He's a Daemon who will appear in the incense's smoke occasionally. So be watchful of how the incense smokes acts when you call on Mammon. I have had the smoke rise a few inches, then flatten out as if a hand was over it, then the smoke would drift towards me. I have my altar in a basement, with no open windows or air sources, to it's not a draft moving the incense smoke.

Mammon and the Law of Attraction

Find images that represent wealth, and combine them with Mammon's sigil. Place his sigil in the center and arrange the other images around the sigil. Use gold or silver glitter glue sticks to make a pattern of gold surrounding your desires, then add a photo of yourself to this, as if you are having all this wealth flow to you.

With an affirmation, incorporate Mammon's ENN and sigil, and know he will bring you what you desire with little fuss or bother.

Pathworking Mammon

This is like all the other pathworkings. Find a quiet spot to settle in, relax yourself, and visualize the following images:

- A bright star in the night sky
- The full moon shining on a landscape of snow
- The sun rising, golden light shining brightly on the landscape
- Drops of golden light falling around you.

Look around. Mammon is with you. Ask him for help in manifesting your desire.

Visualize what you want to have happen, as if it has already manifested. Hold on to these images, breathing deeply.

At this point, see if Mammon communicates with you.

Ask him to depart and to please come when you next call to him.

Chapter 11

Lucifuge

Lucifuge - is it "LOO-SIF-UGE"? Or is it "LUUCY-FOOGE"?

Don't worry. I'm certain I'm not pronouncing his name properly, either. Either way I say it, he shows up and we get stuff done.

I have Lucifuge as part of my "Daemonic Money" class, and I use him quite a bit when working rituals designed to bring money-making opportunities to myself or a client. This is because he is not only Prime Minister of the Underworld (AKA, Hell) but also in charge of the treasury! (He shares this title with Mammon.) He is one of Lucifer's most staunch supporters, and often is tasked with handling matters for Lucifer.

He is known for being a difficult daemon to summon. In fact, one source has this supposed quote from Lucifuge: "Impressive that you summoned me. I am the Tyrant

Lucifuge. Remember that name well!"

In my working with him, I have found him very easy to get along with, if not eager to assist me in my workings.

The key is to be bold with Lucifuge. Not cocky, but summon him with strong intent and be willing to meet him "eye-to-eye", the way one would show confidence when shaking someone's hand, a firm grip and eye-to-eye contact.

Standard Ritual

When working a standard ritual, his ENN is "**Eyen tasa valocur Lucifuge Rofocale**" The suggested pronunciation is "Eh-yen tah-sa val-o-cur Loo-sif-uge Row-fo-kal".

His favorite incense, when I call on him, is a mix of frankincense and dragon's blood.

Suggested offerings are Frankincense resin burned, drop of blood on his sigil - burned, small glass of whiskey or other spirit, raw egg, burned meat.

Lucifuge and the Law of Attraction

This is where he can really help. You can call on him to assist you in figuring out what you desire and how to phrase it. His name can really power up an affirmation, and his sigil on a vision board will bring his powers to manifest what is on the board.

You can ask him to assist you in focusing and visualizing your desire materializing before you, and them to assist you in finding channels for that desire to come to you. He can place you in the right place and time to make a needed contact for a project or he can steer you to the right company so you can get ahead in your profession. If you are self-employed, he can make sure your promotional efforts really pay off.

Pathworking Lucifuge

Just as with the other pathworkings, work when you know you will not be disturbed.

When ready, close your eyes and visualize the following:

- Wooden bench on a dirt path
- Sparkling dew on leaves
- Gold flecks falling in the light
- A starburst of light, getting brighter

Lucifuge should now be with you. He typically walks out of the bright starlight, like a character in a movie walking away from an explosion. It's pretty cool, actually.

Visualize what you want to have happen, as if it has already manifested. Hold on to these images, breathing deeply.

Present your request and then allow him to leave.

Chapter 12

Marbas

Marbas is an excellent choice for dealing with potential enemies, but he is also quite useful in projecting a new vision of yourself to others, such as glamor and beauty, plus he is quite helpful in assisting you in learning new skills rapidly.

He is described in the traditional texts as being a "Great President" of hell, and will sometimes appear as a lion. Illustrations show a humanoid shaped lion, with a fancy waistcoat and human hands. Interesting visual which will come in handy in making a vision board.

Personally, I have used Marbas when dealing with negative people who wish to block me, either out of jealousy or malice. Marbas can, literally, remove the other person's power to block you or cause you harm. He works.

If you need to learn a new language, or learn carpentry, he is an excellent choice to assist you in this. It appears that Marbas can reach across the potential timelines and tap into a version of yourself that has already achieved this skill, and literally install that skill into you.

Potential timelines are where the future appears to split off into two or more tracks, each a result of a specific decision you will, or have already made and events are lined up to occur. This factors into the many worlds theory, where at each major decision you make, there is a world where you decided one way, then another world where you had made a different decision. I do not think this occurs with every decision you make, like deciding on which burger to order at the drive-through. Only major decisions. This has been illustrated for me through many dreams where it seems I am picking up my other life in another timeline. Although this hasn't driven me to drink, I can see where pondering too long on this would make one reach for a bottle of adult beverage.

Marbas's power to remove the ability of someone's magick power was introduced to me via a book on using both angels and demons in a combine ritual. I have sense taken this idea a lot further.

Standard Ritual

To work a standard ritual, this works best for Marbas.

His ENN is "Renach tasa uberace biasa icar Marbas" You say this three times and then ask Marbas to please join with you.

His incense is frankincense. Perhaps mixed with something like white copal, or amber. You can always use a stick of frankincense.

His color is orange, and preferred offerings are alcohol and raw eggs. A blood offering is not usually required.

If you wish to link a specific day or hour to Marbas, he is ruled by the planet Mercury, which is Wednesday and during the hour of Mercury.

Marbas and the Law of Attraction

As I noted in the introduction to Marbas, we can use the imagery of a lion to link any vision boards to Marbas, as well as his unique sigil found in this book.

Place the image of Marbas in the center of a vision board, surrounded by the images of the item you wish to manifest.

In your affirmations book, write the affirmation so that you are asking Marbas to work on the issue on your behalf.

Pathworking Marbas

As always, use a quiet room where you will not be

disturbed. Then visualize the following:

- A golden orb floating in front of you.
- The orb expands and blooms outward like the sun
- Tall oaks in the fall, their orange leaves fall around you
- A path leading to a park bench
- Go and take a seat on the bench

Marbas will then appear, seated next to you on the bench. Talk to him mentally, and present your desire, asking for help in making it manifest. Visualize what you want to have happen, as if it has already manifested. Hold on to these images, breathing deeply.

After communicating with Marbas, end the ritual by standing up, and walk away.

Chapter 13

Volac (also Valac, Ualac, Valax)

There's isn't a lot to say about this Daemon. He's one of the 72 beings in the Ars Goetia, and is listed as a "Mighty President".

If you read the material on Volac, it appears summoning this fellow to be difficult. But, like with the dark Sun Daemon, Sorath, Volac arrives when I work a summoning to him.

He's my "go-to" Daemon for when I need fast cash flow. He's very good at helping you find additional sources of income, perhaps even a change of jobs, as well as help win at gambling. Although, he hasn't helped me in winning a major jackpot, only the occasional small win, and this is when I work a fast ritual right before I buy a lottery ticket.

If I remember to do that!

When I win, I'll give him a small offering, so he knows I'm grateful.

He is described as a winged young boy on a two-headed dragon. So, dragon imagery factors into all aspects of working with Volac. He loves it when you refer to him as "Mister President" but also "Lord" is a good salutation.

It's interesting to note, by Furies fantasy series has the bad guys riding winged dragons, as a kind of infernal air force.

Standard Ritual

Like the others, a basic ritual to Volac involves crafting a petition, and in this case, address the petition to "President Volac" and refer to him formally.

The incense he prefers is a blend of dragon's blood with copal and a base of sandalwood. Or you can source some Japanese incense sicks, in sandalwood or frankincense. Morning Star is my favorite brand, the sticks are wonderful, and it's not too expensive.

Associate him with the planet Jupiter, which means work with him on a Thursday, but that's not a solid requirement. I have found he works well at anytime I summon him.

His preferred offerings are (again) alcohol in the form of a wine or expensive scotch whiskey. He has requested nothing else, but that might change when you summon him.

After setting up and casting your circle, say his ENN

three times, followed by "President Volac, please join with me in my circle". This phrasing is more in line with traditional summonings, so try to stick with this.

Present your petition, then ask him to energize it with his energy. Later, you'll keep this petition in your affirmation book.

Once this is done, give him the offering and place it on his printed sigil on your altar.

Ask him to kindly depart, and to please return when next called upon.

And you're done. Pour the offering out onto the ground, avoiding any plants as the alcohol might harm them.

Volac and the Law of Attraction

Using him with Affirmations is a must. As instructed above, place the petition into this book. Draw his sigil onto the petition, and just keep it there in between the pages.

With a vision board, incorporate Volac's sigil and the imagery of someone riding a dragon. For a vision board, as you place photos of your desire, also place the desire as a sigil mixed with the other images.

Pathworking Volac

Pathworking Volac is like all the other pathworkings.

Find a quiet spot to settle in, relax yourself, and visualize the following images:

- A rocky cliff looming overhead.
- A strange and twisted tree surrounded by bushes.
- A stream of silver begins to drip from the tree.
- Watch the stream of silver flows towards you.

At this point, Volac is with you. Remember to address him as "Mister President" or "My Lord", ask him for his help in manifesting your desire. Visualize what you want to have happen, as if it has already manifested. Hold on to these images, breathing deeply.

Volac will communicate back to you and give thanks to him for helping.

At this point, ask him to depart and you walk away from the silver stream.

Chapter 14

Law of Attraction Specific Rituals

What follows is a master list of the combination of Law of Attraction rituals for multiple topics. I'll list the suitable beings for each type of ritual, but you are not limited to use a specific being for ANY specific ritual. Clauneck is good for wealth, but you can also work a ritual to Verrine for wealth. Call upon Satan for anything, as he's good at speeding up magick.

Work the ritual at any time, as this type of magick is not restricted by time/place/moon phase/planetary positions.

Each Law of Attraction ritual will also have its own specific sigil. Craft your own sigils for each ritual. You are not limited in any way working this magick.

Opening Up to Receive

This may be the easiest exercise to work, or the hardest. It all depends on your point of view. If you have been having trouble manifesting your desire, there may be an issue with your ability to truly receive that which you are trying to manifest. The key is to break free from this deeply ingrained thought pattern.

For this, we can use the pathworking method. I highly recommend you practice doing this, holding the visuals from the beginning of this book, until you are very comfortable in experiencing the practice visuals.

Once you are ready, then you can work this Law of Attraction exercise to remove the negative thought cycles.

We'll be using Marbas for this, as he is quite good at assisting humans in learning new skills, and learning to accept what you are manifesting is an important magick skill to gain.

I recommend working this exercise several times before working any other ritual.

Get into a quiet space and relax.

Visualize the Marbas Pathworking:

- A golden orb floating in front of you.
- The orb expands and blooms outward like the sun
- Tall oaks in the fall, their orange leaves fall

around you
- A path leading to a park bench
- Take a seat on the bench

While seated, call to Marbas in your mind. He should either arrive as if he is walking to you, or he'll simply appear beside you. It's like two people meeting up in the park.

Communicate with him, talk to him. Be open. Be honest. Ask for his help in learning to accept what you deserve, what you are manifesting.

Try to listen when he gives you advice. You may not actually receive his voice, you may just get a shift in your emotions. Sit for a moment in silence. After that, visualize the joy of your desire arriving. Don't worry about HOW it arrives, just that is HAS arrived.

After a few minutes, let those images go, and repeat to yourself the following phrase:

"I am worthy of happiness, health, and riches. I open up to receive daily. Marbas is cleansing me of old, outdated programming and I am now receiving my greatest desire. Thank you, Marbas!"

Hold this a minute, then stand up from the bench. Turn to Marbas, and thank him for his help.

Open your eyes and this exercise is finished.

Law of Attraction Rituals for Wealth

When manifesting money, wealth, a rise in income, there are several daemons to choose from. Of the list in this book, in no particular order, you can summon Satan, Clauneck, Lucifuge, Mammon, or Volac.

The Law of Attraction methods typically involve the use of affirmations, vision boards, and visualization.

Incorporating a Daemon into your LOA wealth manifestations is really simple and straightforward.

Starting with an Affirmation, this is a decent template you can use:

"I now have large amounts of money flowing to me, and with the assistance of (Daemon's name), this money

flow increases and increases every day. I give thanks to (Daemon's name) for granting me my desire, and I allow the money to flow to me without restrictions."

Write your affirmation, with any small edits from the statement above, into your notebook reserved for Affirmations. You then add the Daemon's sigil below the Affirmation.

Working the Affirmation

Daily, for the next several weeks, when you know you can be undisturbed, open the book to the Affirmation, read what you have written, then close your eyes and visualize the Daemon being with you, and see money and gold coins flowing towards you. Hold this for a few moments, then whisper the Affirmation to yourself.

Take a deep breath, silently thank the Daemon, and close the book.

Making a Vision Board

This is pretty straightforward. Get a small corkboard or poster board, some tacks or tape, glue, whatever you have handy to stick the pictures to the corkboard or poster board.

Hit up Google and search for images of money, gold,

luxury cars and houses. Things that represent to you the idea of wealth.

Hunt for an image that represents the idea of poverty.

Print out the images you have found. Set the ones representing money and wealth aside for now. Pick up the image of poverty. Using a red pen or marker (even a crayon works) and draw a huge "X" over the image. Across the image, write "I banish POVERTY!"

Set this aside.

Print out a sigil to the daemon. Make sure it's an activated sigil.

Set the board on a table. Past or pin the sigil to the center. Next, begin attaching the images of wealth to the board.

On the BACK of the board, tape the banishment of poverty in the center.

Stare at the board, and silently do a pathworking to summon your chosen Daemon. Ask them to activate the images on the vision board, bringing the energy of wealth to you and into you. Visualize now the money and luxury items flowing to you, and see yourself in the luxury car and house. Thank the Damon for their help and let them know you're done for now.

Put this vision board anywhere, but it's best to make sure others won't see it, as their disbelief may work to dilute or stop the magick. I put mine in a closet I open daily.

Just look at the vision board as often as you can, and do a fast visual of the Daemon bringing you all this wealth.

Custom Sigil

Here's where we get a bit into classic Chaos Magick.

You can craft a sigil that incorporates your desire AND chosen Daemon into a single bit of abstract art that will act as a magick talisman. To do this, we need to condense your affirmation statement into as few words as possible. My favorite is to simply state *"(Daemon's Name) brings to me great wealth, money and cash, in ever greater amounts daily."*

Use a statement like this to craft a sigil. My High Magick 101 workbook has worksheets to assist you in this, and I'll attach an outline for sigil creation in the Appendix of this book. Of course, you can use ANY statement you desire. This is just an example. The entire statement MUST be as short as possible, as the sigil from a lengthy statement can look like a hot mess, and just a mess of lines or letter. Aim for a sleek, clean design.

Once this sigil is created, you can draw it with your Affirmation or attach it to your vision board.

Standard Wealth Ritual

I'm including this to give you a contrasting choice when working wealth magick, or manifesting wealth. Leading up to this ritual, you will need to choose a Daemon to summon and work with, and craft your statement of desire and a sigil.

This ritual is designed for beginners, and I figure a seasoned practitioner would find working this as a refresher in the basics of High Magick.

To begin, assemble the following items. This is a "bare bones" list. To this, you can add most anything you think will help enhance the ritual.

You will need:

- **Two white candles.**
- **A money draw candle (Gold if possible, or green otherwise)**
- **Incense. Go with a good brand, most any fragrance. I use resins. Frankincense is best, otherwise go with any clearing type of incense.**
- **The Daemon's Sigil**
- **A statement of desire (details on what to say follows this list)**
- **An offering. ANY Daemon will be happy with a small glass of wine, but you**

can also offer an egg or a bit of nature. If you wish, you may also offer a drop of blood. Do so by using a lance device and placing a drop of blood on their sigil.

- **Four or five of pieces of currency. Or large coins. In the US, go with a half-dollar if possible. (These will be used later.)**

Once you have your statement and sigil, you are ready to work the ritual. Start with lighting the incense. If using charcoal, make sure you have time for the charcoal to be completely covered in ash before beginning. Allow the incense to produce smoke.

Light all white candles.

Turn off room lights.

Cast a circle as described in the Appendix.

Take a moment to center yourself and relax. Several deep breaths.

Say the Daemon's ENN three times, then ask the Daemon to join with you. Try to detect the Daemon's presence. Don't worry if you can't feel them. They'll be there.

Example:

> *Tasa reme laris Satan – Ave Satanis*
> *Tasa reme laris Satan – Ave Satanis*
> *Tasa reme laris Satan – Ave Satanis*

Satan, please join with me now.

Pick up the statement of desire. Read it aloud. Phrase it like this example:

Satan, I humbly ask that you assist me in building great wealth! I ask that you guide me and bring to me the opportunities to generate great wealth. I thank you for your help!

Pick up the gold (or green) candle. Hold it up and say,

I ask that you now energize and charge this candle with your energy to draw to me great wealth!

Place the candle into a sturdy candle holder and light it. This candle will need to burn completely. I use small chime candles in solid glass holders that are left after burning scented candles.

Pick up the coins, and hold them in your hands. Say:

I ask that you energize these coins to draw money to me, money in ever-increasing amounts.

At this time, pick up the offering. If it's an egg, hold it in both hands. A glass of wine, hold the glass up as if making a toast.

I humbly ask you to accept this small offering in gratitude for your kind assistance.

Sit the offering on the Daemon's sigil.

The ritual is complete. Ask the Daemon to depart as follows:

(Daemon's name), I thank you for being with me in my space. You may depart now and please return when I next call upon you.

To finish the ritual, pick up the money. These coins or paper money are now magnets for money. Keep one with you in your pocket or purse. Make sure NOT to spend it. Take one and place it under your front door (hidden or buried). Place another in your bedroom, under the head of your bed. The 4th can be placed where you work or in your vehicle.

Law of Attraction Ritual for Health

For this, you will use Verrine or Astaroth, but you can certainly use Satan or another Daemon, as their powers are not limited by humans. Manifesting good health or healing follows the basics I outlined in the section on manifesting money and wealth.

Remember, magick and the Law of Attraction is not a substitute for the advice and care of a medical professional. Verrine will assist you in obtaining the correct diagnoses, the proper treatment, and even to the point of assisting you with a healthier diet and exercise.

Affirmations

Working with your Affirmation book, I suggest you start with a short affirmation that asks the Daemon's help in healing, either yourself or someone else close to you. I'm using Verrine in this example, but you can change this to use Astaroth, or any other Daemon you wish to use. Use the following as a template and change it to match your circumstances.

"I am now healthy, I have no illness in my body and my body grows stronger and healthier day after day, and with the assistance of (Daemon's name), I am now at the peak of health, and I radiate healthy energy. I give thanks to (Daemon's name) for granting me superb health and vitality."

Combine this with Verrine's sigil in your Affirmation book.

You can use that affirmation as a template for a custom sigil. Use as few words as possible for a sigil, making sure to use the Daemon's name.

A suggestion would be:

"I am now healthy and fit, thanks to (Daemon)."

This is all that is needed for a special sigil. Again, refer to the sigil instructions in the Appendix of this book.

Vision Board

Use a small poster board. Collect some images of people in good health, patients being with doctors, and general scenes that depict robust health and vitality.

Under the images, put the phrase "I am healthy" several times, and place Verrine's sigil in each corner. You can also put the sigil you made on this board, giving that sigil a nice boost in magick energy.

David Thompson

Law of Attraction Ritual for Love/Relationships

Possibly the most difficult type of manifestation to achieve. Although any desire that involves the cooperation of others is difficult. It's hard to generate a genuine emotional response in others, and often the targets of this type of magick may not even be capable of returning any emotions you may be feeling.

To this end, and this is always my recommendation, use this type of ritual to make yourself emanate the aura of love, of glamor, and to place you in the path of that other person. If you don't have your eye on another, this can be used to help encounter a potential lover or life companion.

However, working this will have no effect if you have

no desire to get out and allow yourself to be led to situations where that person can be encountered. Your future soul-mate won't be dropped off by the post office onto your doorstep. You have to meet the magick half-way.

The best Daemons for this desire would be Astaroth, followed by Marbas, to project an image of a more glamorous version of yourself.

There are two directions to go when working magick for love and relationships. Are you wanting to attract someone new? Or do you wish to rekindle the flames of desire in an existing relationship?

Ages ago, I had a distant relative who rekindled her marriage. According to my uncle, what she did was to obtain some adult magazines from various sources, possibly from my uncle, and she went to work cutting various sexy pictures out and into an envelope.

One day, her husband comes home to find a centerfold taped to the front door. Pictures were on the floor, of various revealing photos of hot models. He follows this trail, and he finds bits of lingerie with the photos. He was getting pretty worked up when he saw the bedroom door closed, and a very revealing centerfold taped to the door.

He opens the door to find his wife lying in bed, ready for action.

Yes, this rekindled the relationship. It was also a

source of laughter with my uncle and grandmother.

You don't need magick to rekindle, but this was a type of magick that worked, and they didn't even know they were working magick. She enchanted her husband using images designed to get his motor running.

If attracting a new partner, define their traits you wish them to have. Just be cautious in doing this, as you don't want to get so picky Astaroth can't put you in the path of someone.

Sigils and Rituals

To attract a new relationship, or even just a new fling, let's look at creating an aura of glamor and appeal for yourself, add a dose of self-confidence, mix in with some attraction oil (any come-to-me oil works), then ask Astaroth enchant your energy with that of love, projecting this love, which will attract potential partners to you like moths to a porch light in August in Texas.

It's pretty simple.

Craft a petition that asks Astaroth to assist you in projecting love energy. Work her ritual with pink candles, a custom sigil using your affirmation (next) and some oils.

Affirmations

Pretty much the same pattern as with the affirmations for wealth applies here.

Word an affirmation like this sample:

"I ask Astaroth to assist me in projecting the aura of love, to assist me in filling my energy with the pink light of love, beauty, and glamor. With her help, I now attract (men or women) who are a perfect fit for me. With Astaroth's help, they find me irresistible and alluring." Or words to that effect.

Write this in your Affirmation Book, along with Astaroth's sigil. Or simplify the phrase into as few of words as possible and create a sigil.

Vision Board Ideas

Depending on your ultimate goal, a vision board can either be just some generic images of people "being couples" and the usual sunset walks on the beach (with or without a loyal canine companion), couples at dinner, and even a wedding. You can go so far as to cut and paste your face over the people in the images.

You should print out the sigil for the Daemon you're working with on this desire. Place their sigil on the vision board, along with the custom sigil.

To this board, you can add the color pink, for love,

and the color red, for passion.

Chapter 15

The New Daemonic Sigils

Ten new sigils follow.

There is also a link to my website where you can download the set in Adobe Acrobat, ready to be printed on standard sized paper by any printer. There will be multiple sizes on each page, so you can have a sigil for the ritual, and one to carry around, and one to hang on a wall.

Once you have the sigils printed, you need to activate them. I advise activating one set at a time, as you need them. If you need to print more, you also need to activate the new set. Most any artisan can create a metal talisman from any of these sigils, and you are free to do so. Just don't make dozens and try to sell them.

Activation

To activate a sigil, or talisman created from a sigil, go

into your space, and prepare your altar in any way that suits you. When ready, light candles and incense. You will need any purifying incense. I use frankincense here because I have a lot of it handy and it works.

Collect all versions of the sigil.

When the incense is going, begin with reciting the Daemon's ENN, or call to them using pathworking.

Ask them to charge and activate the sigil.

Pass each one through the incense smoke. Allow the smoke to touch both sides.

With the last sigil, place them all out on your altar and gaze at them.

Again, ask the Daemon to charge the sigils, and continue to gaze at them for a few breaths.

You're done. You may move on with a ritual, or stop at this point. Room lights on, and candles snuffed out.

Satan Sigil

Satan

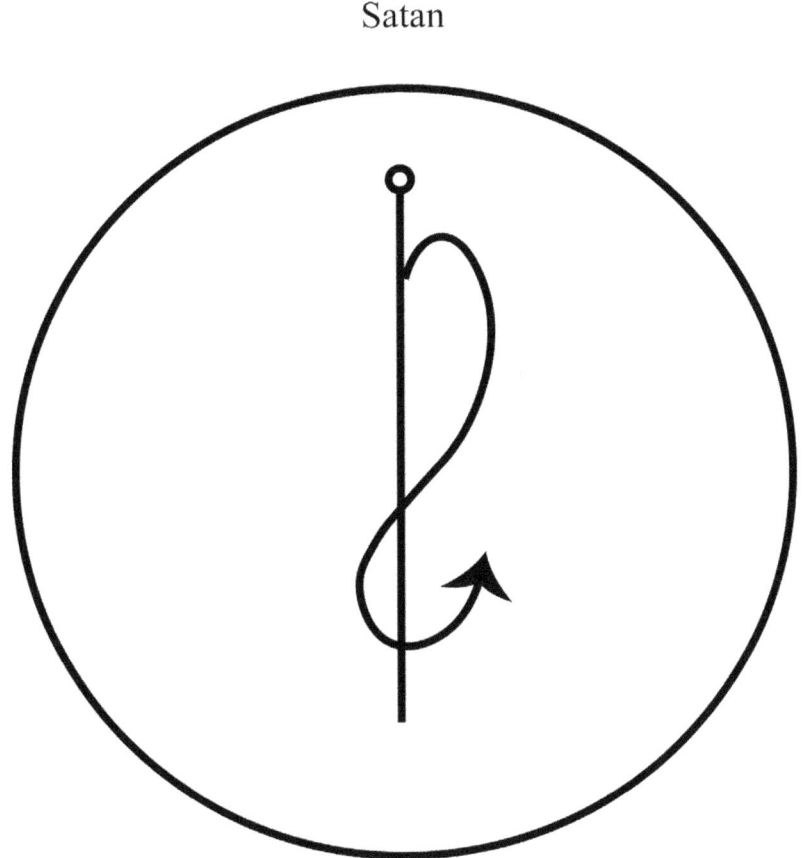

David Thompson

Clauneck Sigil

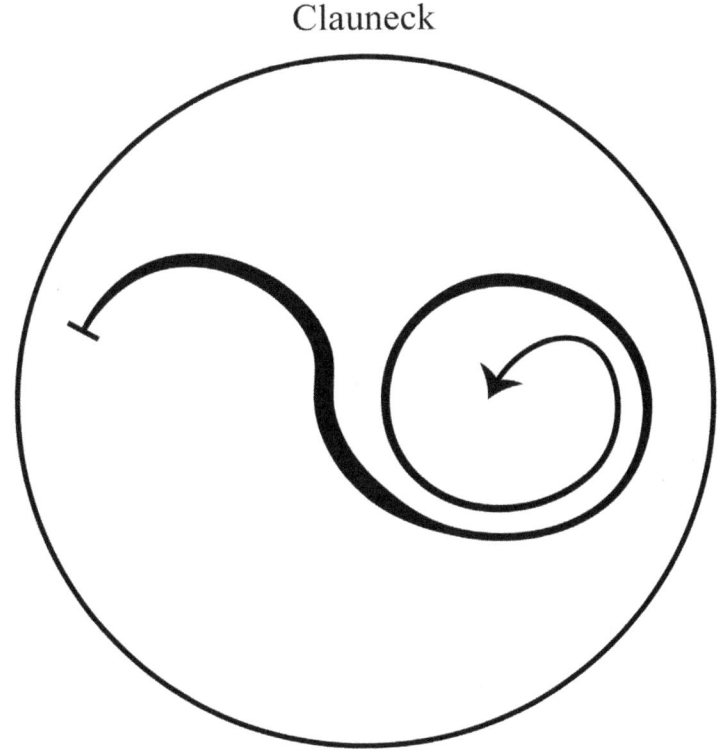

David Thompson

Astaroth Sigil

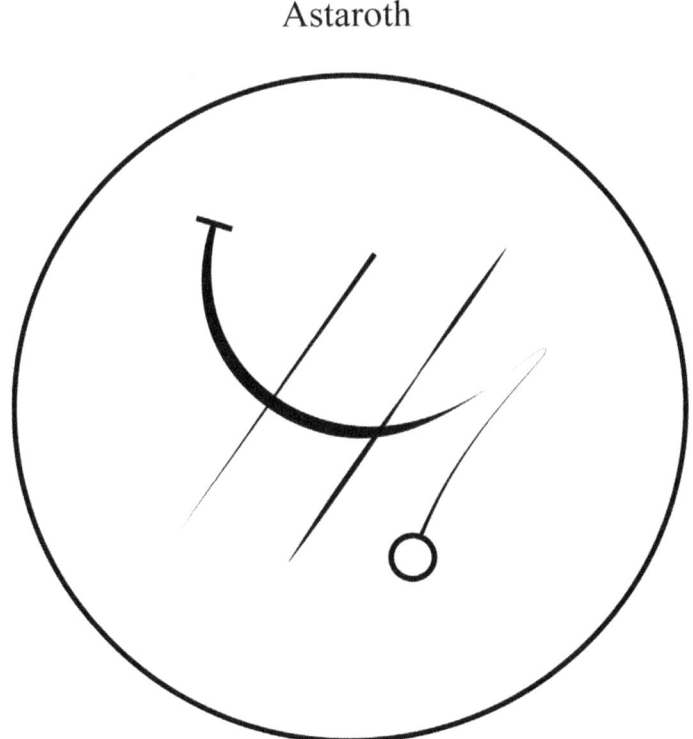

David Thompson

Seer Sigil

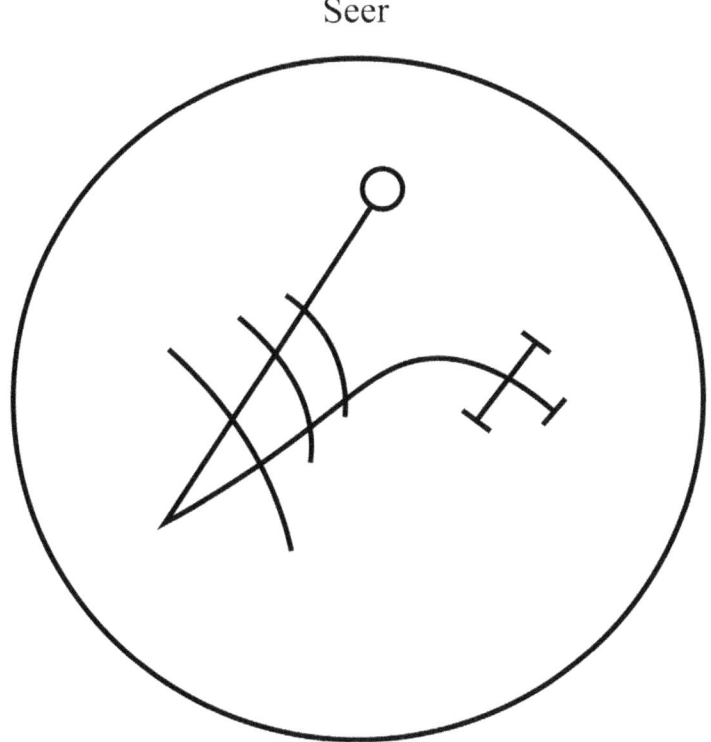

David Thompson

Flereous Sigil

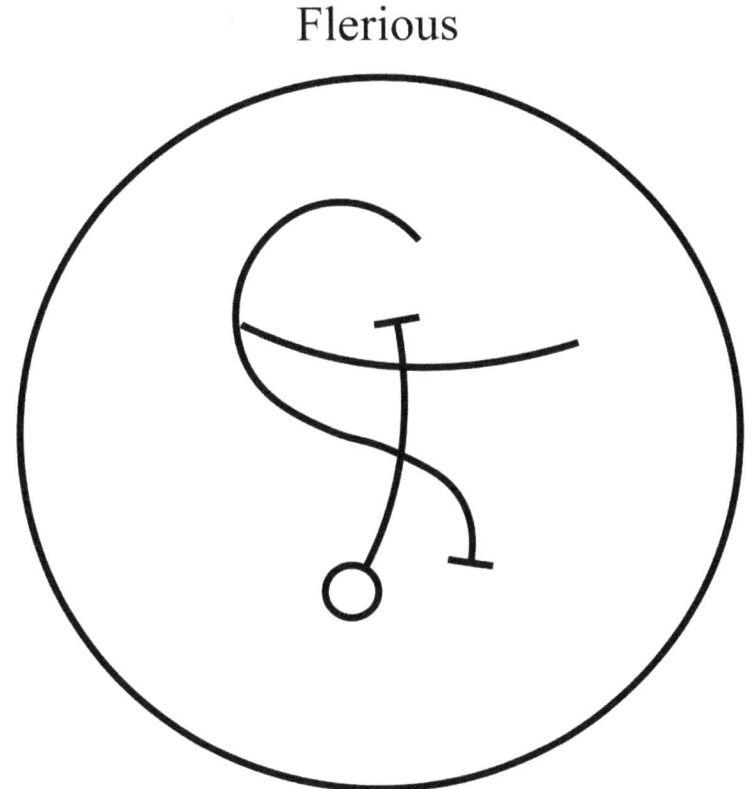

David Thompson

Verrine Sigil

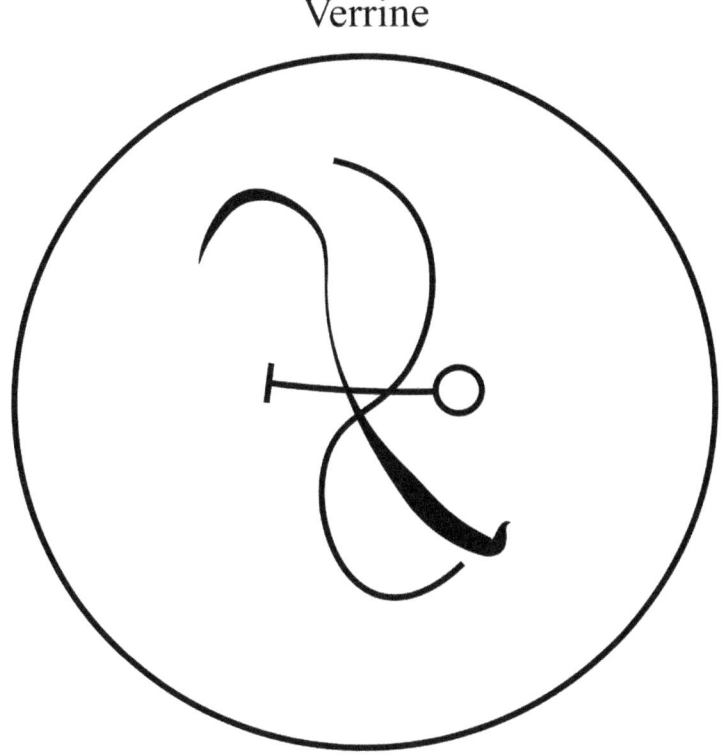

David Thompson

Mammon

Mammon

David Thompson

Lucifuge

David Thompson

Marbas

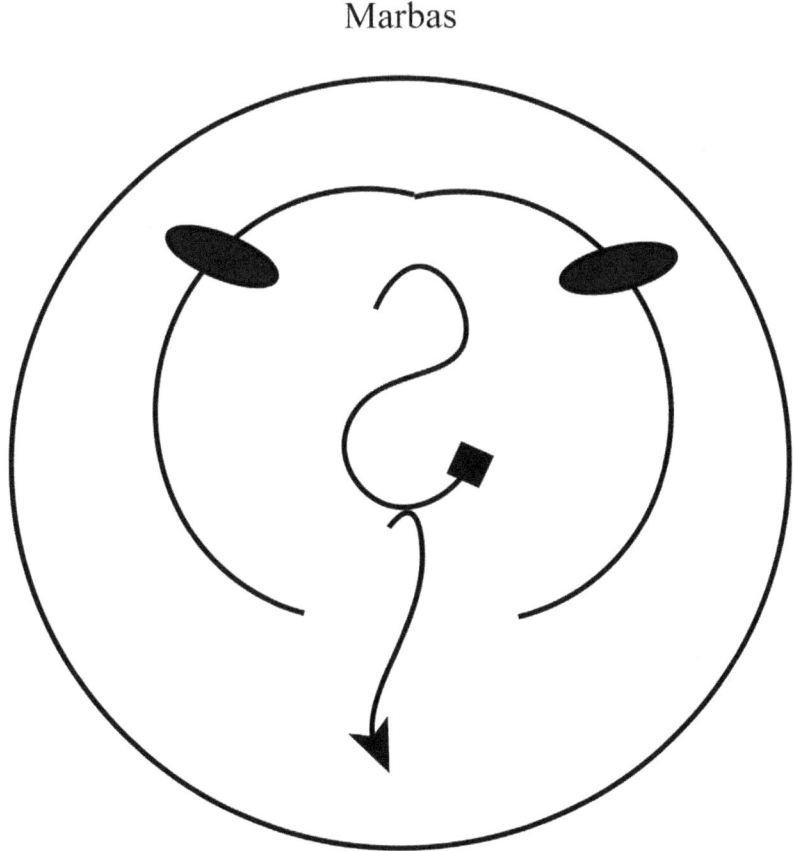

David Thompson

Volac

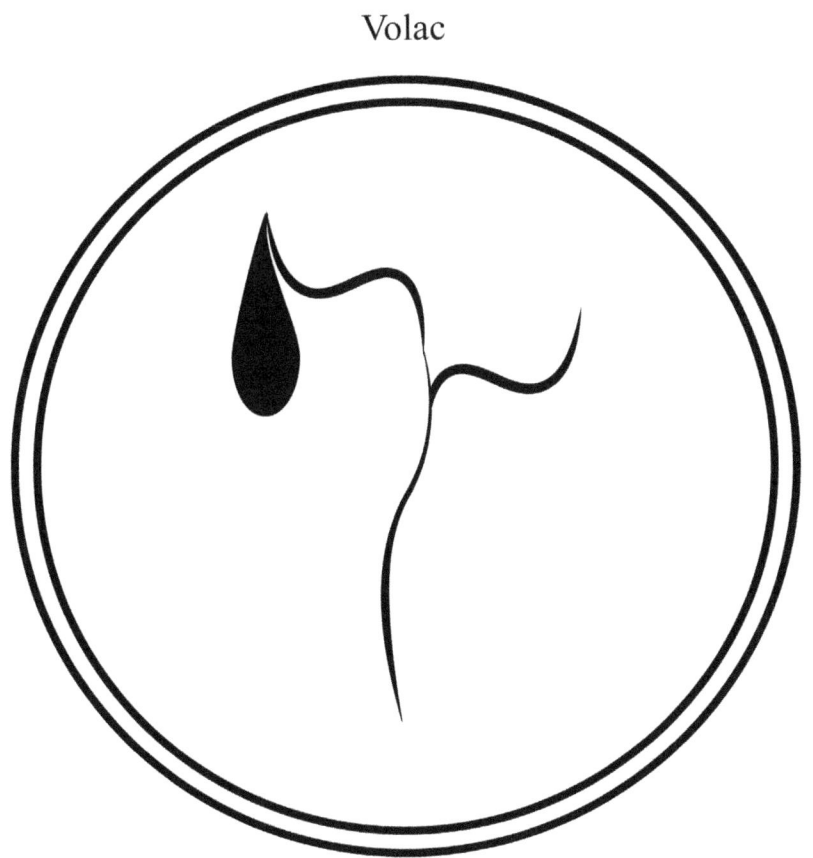

Appendix

Hacking the Law of Attraction class.

This book is based upon my class, and acts as a supplement to this class.

I normally give this class "live" using Zoom lectures, but since I am now limiting all "live" classes to one a year, I made several of my classes available as a replay.

It's not required to take this class, but if you feel it'll assist you in manifesting your desire, I have included the link to the replay class below. You will get instant access to a set of downloads, and you can view the lectures on your device at any time.

If you use the code DAEMONSLOA you'll get 10% off this class.

https://davepsychic.com/classes/hacking-loa-3-2/

The ENNS

Demonic Enns are calls of invitation, admiration, or protection to certain Demons that are chanted, vibrated, or spoken for Demonic Evocation.

I'll list all the ENNs for the Daemons in this book here in one spot for easy reference:

Satan – Tasa reme laris Satan – Ave Satanis
Clauneck - Ahvalen Esen Clauneck Kiar
Ashtaroth – Tasa Alora foren Ashtaroth
Seer – Jeden et Renich Seer tu tasa
Flereous – Ganic Tasa Fubin Flereous
Verrine – Elan Typan Verrine
Mammon – Tasa Mammon on ca lirach
Lucifuge – Eyen tasa valocur Lucifuge Rofocale
Marbas – Renich tasa uberaca biasa icar Marbas
Volac - Avage Secore on ca Volac

Some of these ENNs may not be what you're used to seeing, especially for Clauneck, but it was what was given to me when I questioned him about his calling phrase.

Circle Casting

This is a revision of my usual instructions on how to cast a circle. The changes are based upon many emails and messages.

Standard Circle Casting

Traditional circles are cast by walking around your altar, first facing north, then to the east, moving clockwise. One invokes the elements, or guardians, of each direction. Traditional Daemonolatry has one draw a specific shape in the air with a finger or athame (knife) or wand.

My standard circle combines all of that and makes it fairly simple. You are still creating a circle of energy designed to keep energy out and invite positive energy in.

For this, I always start the frankincense going. It's very useful to reset the energies in your space. Especially if you use good quality resin or sticks.

Optional: Using a wand or athame. I use my finger, works just as well.

Face North. Deep breath, then walk clockwise around your space, tracing an invisible line with your finger, so that the line encompasses all the space. Once you have walked the circle, face north again.

If your altar is against a wall, or you can't walk around the entire space, VISUALIZE the circle expanding out to totally surround your space, and walk a smaller circle on one side of your altar.

Address the element Earth, represented by the Daemon Belial, face NORTH and say:

Lirach Tasa Vefa Wehlic, Belial

Address the element Air, represented by the Daemon Lucifer, face EAST and say:

Renich Tasa Uberaca Biasa Icar, Lucifer

Address the element Fire, represented by the Daemon Flereous, face SOUTH and say:

Ganic Tasa fubin, Flereous

Address the element Water, represented by the Daemon Leviathan, face WEST and say:

Jedan Tasa hoet naca, Leviathan

Now you have evoked the elements.

In your mind, visualize a bright circle of orange light enveloping your space. In your mind, see this light expanding to create a column of light all around you, extending up into the air and into space, and down into the earth, to the planet's core.

You are now ready to start your ritual.

The "standard" Daemonolatry method adds the tracing of the Z-D sigil in the air when facing each direction. Trace the letter "Z" in the air, then circle the "Z" with a "D" by extending the bottom bit of the "Z" up and around to make the "D", then draw your finger down.

You may also trace out a pentagram in the air. It's totally up to you.

Ejecting the unwanted energies:

This is the most important step. The last thing you need in your circle is unwanted, negative energies. These energies will interfere with the magick and cause unwanted and unexpected results if it doesn't completely derail the whole thing.

After the circle, I will make a sweeping motion with my out-stretched hands, as if I was gathering up energy and then I'll "toss" the energies out of the space, usually saying:

"All unwanted and invited energies must depart the space now!" You may add any other descriptive phrases that suit you, such as "Begone Jerks!", etc.

Simplified Method:

If you have a private altar space that is not subject to others entering it, then after the first method above, the subsequent rituals may begin with a very simplified cast.

I will face north and visualize the ring of gold energy appearing, surrounding my space, and forming a solid cylinder.

Then I'll simply call on the elements, by turning to

face that direction, but without walking around with my finger tracing out the circle.

I still say the ENNs, and call in the Daemons.

Pathworking Method:

This method is to simply sit, and visualize each element arriving, and forming the magick circle. I do this by imagining a small stream forming around me, followed by air swirling over the water, then followed by the water turning to fire, which blazes and forms bricks.

Next are the other circle methods I've included in my other books.

Color Correspondences

Here are the meanings of different candle colors in general:

- White candles-Destruction of negative energy, peace, truth and purity
- Purple candles- Spiritual awareness, wisdom, tranquility
- Lavender Candles– Intuition, Paranormal, Peace, Healing
- Blue and Deep Blue Candles– Meditation, Healing, Forgiveness, Inspiration, Fidelity, Happiness, and opening lines of Communication.
- Green Candles– Money, Fertility, Luck, Abundance, Health (not to be used when diagnosed with Cancer), Success
- Rose and Pink Colored Candles– Positive self-love, friendship, harmony, joy
- Yellow Candles- Realizing and manifesting thoughts, opening up communication, confidence, bringing plans into action, creativity, intelligence, mental clarity, clairvoyance.

- Orange Candles– Joy, energy, education, strength attraction, stimulation
- Red or Deep red Candles– Passion, energy, love, lust, relationships, sex, vitality, courage.
- Black Candles– Protection, absorption and destruction of negative energy and also repelling negative energy from others
- Silver candle– Goddess or feminine energy, remove negativity, psychic development, money
- Gold candle– Male energy, Solar energy, fortune, spiritual attainment, money.

Candle colors and Days:

Sunday– Gold or yellow candles

Monday– Silver, Grey or White

Tuesday-Red

Wednesday-Purple

Thursday– Blue

Friday-Green

Saturday– Black or Purple

Days of the week:

Sunday = The day of the Sun. Useful for healing, creativity, success.
Monday = The day of the Moon (Hecate). Travel, fertility, farming, psychic powers.
Tuesday = The day of Mars (Ares). Overcoming challenges, cursing others, psychic attack.
Wednesday = The day of Mercury (Hermes). Magick that needs communication,
Thursday = The day of Jupiter (Zeus). Business, money, wealth, abundance.
Friday = The day of Venus (Aphrodite). Love and family rituals work best this day.
Saturday = The day of Saturn. Banishing, karma retribution, protection, curse breaking.

Moon Phases:

New Moon = Restarts. Work magick intended to bring to you anything.
New Moon to Full Moon (Waxing Moon) = Magick to start a business, garden, romance. Think of this period as the "Bring to me" phase.
Full Moon= Major magick time. Working with a moon goddess (Hecate) at this point in time. Energy builds as the moon grows full, and timing for this is anywhere from two days before the full moon to one day after full moon.
Full Moon towards New Moon (Waning Moon). Magick to release things. Magick to break curses, remove blocks, remove toxic people.

Helpful Links:

Planetary Hour Calculator:
https://www.astrology.com.tr/planetary-hours.asp

Moon Phase Calculator:
https://www.astrology.com.tr/moon-calendar.asp

Link to the Daemon Sigils
https://davepsychic.com/daemonsloasigils/

The Pendulum

Using a pendulum in a ritual is a great way to communicate with the daemon, and hear what they may be trying to tell you.

Have a pendulum chart with you in the circle, and use the pendulum to ask Yes/No questions while in a ritual.

No pendulum? Make one, using a small piece of string and a weight, such as a ring or key. After making the pendulum, activate it and get it ready to be used.

Activating and Charging your Pendulum

Before working the ritual that uses a pendulum, let's first consecrate the pendulum.

To do this, place the pendulum on your workspace and hold your hands over it.

Imagine a light entering your head and flowing into your hands, then into the pendulum.

Now say:

In the name of EH-EI-EH I ask you, Angel METATRON to bless this pendulum and shape its energies for spirit communication with Genius entities. Make it safe for myself while I use this pendulum. So be it! Amein! (That last work is Hebraic for So be IT)

Now, your pendulum is ready for use.

David Thompson

Yes/No Chart

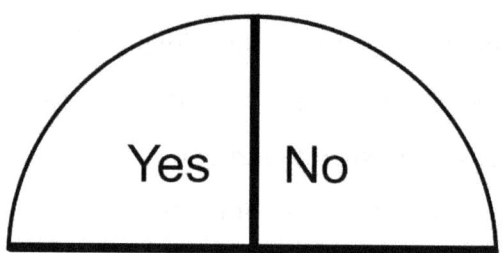

Complex Sigils Creation

Some people will try to convince you that sigil creation is some type of complicated process and is all occult and ultra-top secret.

The information is all out there (meaning the interwebs) so what I am about to show you here isn't new, isn't some wild idea of my own, it's been used for well over 125 years. (Like the term "magick" or "magik", sheesh!)

Once you have a summary of your desire, phrased as a "past tense" statement, you will have a sentence of about 5 to 10 words.

Past tense simply means you phrase a desire as if it has already occurred.

A statement such as "I have one million dollars" would be a good example.

A statement such as "I wish to receive a huge sum of money" isn't. It's in future tense, uses a soft way of asking, "wish" and the money isn't well defined.

Forget about HOW the money will come to you, you already have it.

So, taking this statement, you'd look at what letters exist, then cross out each vowel (and I include the vowel "y" in this).

Thus, the following happens:

David Thompson

I have one million dollars

⬇ Remove Vowels

~~I~~ h~~a~~v~~e~~ ~~o~~n~~e~~ m~~i~~ll~~io~~n d~~o~~ll~~a~~rs

⬇

HVNMLLNDLLRS

⬇ Remove Duplicate Letters

HVNML~~L~~N~~D~~~~L~~~~L~~RS

⬇

HVNMLDRS

Here's the resulting sigil created with those letters:

Nothing fancy, just a design using the letters. I whipped this up in Photoshop, but drawing this by hand is much more effective.

To take this further, you convert the letters to numbers, using any one of a number of translation methods. Once you have the letters converted, you map the numbers on a planetary square to generate a sigil based upon the magick of that planet!

My favorite is the use of the "Jewish Gematria":

Jewish Gematria

A=1	J=600	S=90
B=2	K=10	T=100
C=3	L=20	U=200
D=4	M=30	V=700
E=5	N=40	W=900
F=6	O=50	X=300
G=7	P=60	Y=400
H=8	Q=70	Z=500
I=9	R=80	

Thus, the letters "HVNMLDRS" will become

8, 700, 40, 30, 20, 4, 80, 90

If you look at the magick square of Jupiter, it only goes from 1-12, so you have to reduce the numbers to their lowest logical number. Thus, 700 becomes 7.

Now, we have 8,7,4,3,2,8,9

Overlay this on the Jupiter square:

Base 6 English Gematria

A = 6	**H** = 48	**N** = 84	**U** = 126
B = 12	**I** = 54	**O** = 90	**V** = 132
C = 18	**J** = 60	**P** = 96	**W** = 138
D = 24	**K** = 66	**Q** = 102	**X** = 144
E = 30	**L** = 72	**R** = 108	**Y** = 150
F = 36	**M** = 78	**S** = 114	**Z** = 156
G = 42		**T** = 120	

Draw a large dot over the letter 8, then a line to the rest of the numbers in order as shown.

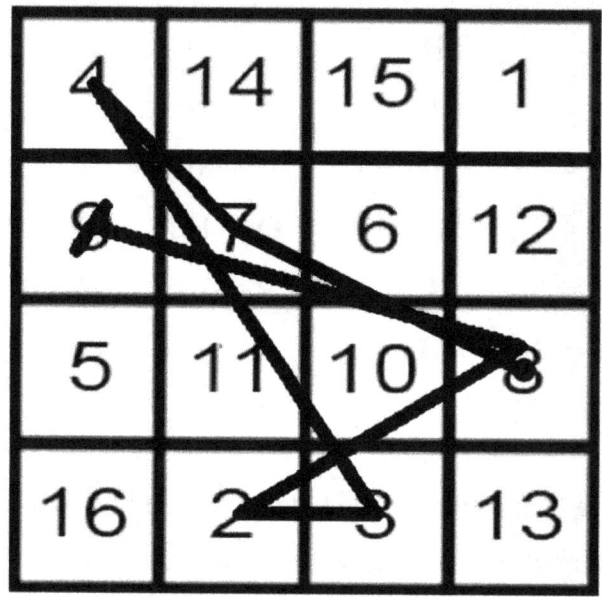

Then take the square away and you have the "working magic sigil"

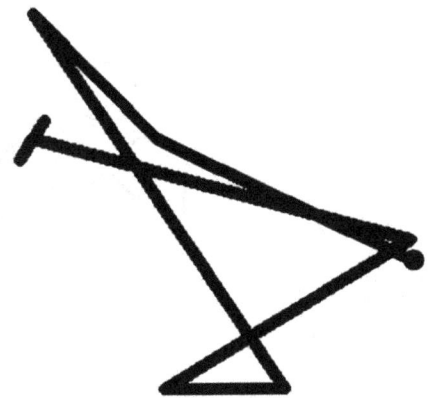

The various planetary squares are next.

THE *KAMEA* OF MERCURY
& PLANETARY SIGILS

8	58	59	5	4	62	63	1
49	15	14	52	53	11	10	56
41	23	22	44	45	19	18	48
32	34	35	29	28	38	39	25
40	26	27	37	36	30	31	33
17	47	46	20	21	43	42	24
9	55	54	12	13	51	50	16
64	2	3	61	60	6	7	57

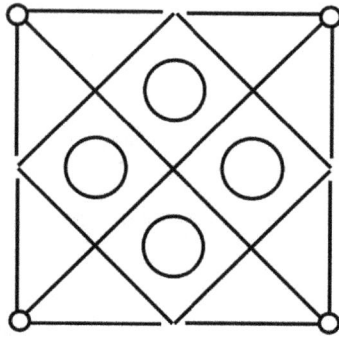

- Each row and column contains eight numbers
- The square contains 64 numbers from 1 to 64
- Each row, column and diagonal adds up to 260.
- All of the numbers in the square add up to 2080

THE *KAMEA* OF VENUS
& PLANETARY SIGILS

22	47	16	41	10	35	4
5	23	48	17	42	11	29
30	6	24	49	18	36	12
13	31	7	25	43	19	37
38	14	32	1	26	44	20
21	39	8	33	2	27	45
46	15	40	9	34	3	28

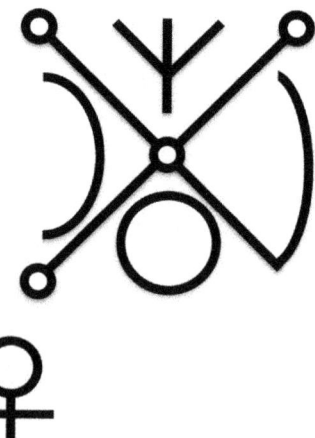

- Each row and column contains seven numbers
- The square contains 49 numbers from 1 to 49
- Each row, column and diagonal adds up to 175.
- All of the numbers in the square add up to 1225

The *Kamea* of Luna & Planetary Sigils

37	78	29	70	21	62	13	54	5
6	38	79	30	71	22	63	14	46
47	7	39	80	31	72	23	55	15
16	48	8	40	81	32	64	24	56
57	17	49	9	41	73	33	65	25
26	58	18	50	1	42	74	34	66
67	27	59	10	51	2	43	75	35
36	68	19	60	11	52	3	44	76
77	28	69	20	61	12	53	4	45

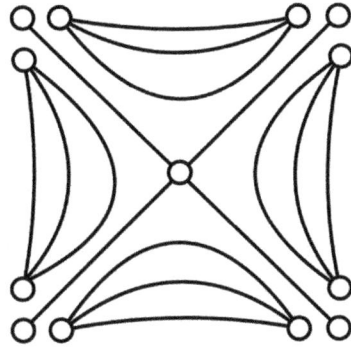

- Each row and column contains nine numbers
- The square contains 81 numbers from 1 to 81
- Each row, column and diagonal adds up to 260.
- All of the numbers in the square add up to 2080

THE KAMEA AND SIGIL OF MARS

11	24	7	20	3
4	12	25	8	16
17	5	13	21	9
10	18	1	14	22
23	6	19	2	15

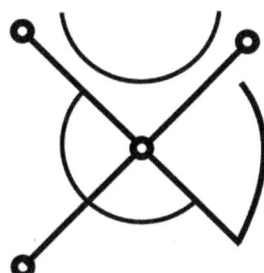

The Sigils or Seals of Mars

The *Kamea*, or Magic Square, of Mars, has the numbers 5, 25, 65, and 325 as its keys:
- Each row, column and diagonal has 5 squares.
- There are 25 boxes, holding 1 through 25
- Each row, column and diagonal adds to 65
- All the numbers add to 325

David Thompson

THE *KAMEA* OF JUPITER & PLANETARY SIGILS

4	14	15	1
9	7	6	12
5	11	10	8
16	2	3	13

- Each row and column contains 4 numbers
- The square contains 16 numbers from 1 to 16
- Each row, column and diagonal adds up to 34.
- All of the numbers in the square add up to 136

The *Kamea* and Seal and Sign of Saturn

4	9	2
3	5	7
8	1	6

ד	ט	ב
ג	ה	ז
ח	א	ו

- Each row and column contains three numbers
- The square contains 9 numbers from 1 to 9
- Each row, column and diagonal adds up to 15.
- All of the numbers in the square add up to 45

THE *KAMEA* OF THE SUN & PLANETARY SIGILS

6	32	3	34	35	1
7	11	27	28	8	30
19	14	16	15	23	24
18	20	22	21	17	13
25	29	10	9	26	12
36	5	33	4	2	31

- Each row and column contains six numbers.
- The square contains 36 numbers from 1 to 36.
- Each row, column and diagonal adds up to 111.
- All of the numbers in the square add up to 666.

About the Author

Dave is an author of adult fantasy (The Furies series) as well as author of occult books about magick.

David began working ritual magick back in the 1970s. He took a brief break, then used the power of this magick to create a photography career which took him to Los Angeles and work as a photographer for multiple magazines.

David has studied magick in all forms, and in 2018, released a three-part magick instruction course in High Magick. Thousands of students have benefited from David's unique teaching style, making ceremonial magick accessible to everyone.

Dave's Facebook Page:
https://www.facebook.com/DavePsychic/

Secrets of Magick Facebook Group:

https://www.facebook.com/groups/secretsofmagick

Join the Grecian Magick Facebook group!
https://www.facebook.com/groups/grecianmagick

And finally, Dave's webpage, book readings and his services:
https://davepsychic.com

Sign-up for my Newsletter and get a FREE E-Book!
https://davepsychic.com/newsletter

Jpeg and a printable PDF of all the sigils is available on my website at
https://davepsychic.com/daemonsloasigils/

www.ingramcontent.com/pod-product-compliance
Lightning Source LLC
Chambersburg PA
CBHW060647150426
42811CB00086B/2451/J